Jean-Luc Aubarbier
Michel Binet

Wonderful
PÉRIGORD

Photographs by Jean-Pierre Bouchard

ÉDITIONS OUEST-FRANCE
13, rue du Breil, Rennes

Introduction

The Dordogne valley, near Beynac.

On the banks of the Dordogne, the castles of Fayrac, on the right, and Castelnaud in the background.

The Vézère valley, a prehistoric royal road, listed "heritage of humanity".

The geography and economy of Périgord

Forming part of the administrative Region of Aquitaine, providing its most northerly fringe, the *département* of Dordogne (9,225 km^2, the third-largest in France in terms of area) sees its present-day borders coincide almost perfectly with the limits of the former province of Périgord. Situated between the crystalline slopes of the foothills of the Massif Central to the north-east and the rich alluvial plains of the Basin of Aquitaine to the south-west, it is chiefly watered by the Dordogne, the Isle, the Dronne and the Vézère. Traditionally a distinction is made between White Périgord (*Périgord Blanc* — around Périgueux and the Isle Valley), Green Périgord (*Périgord Vert* — Ribérac, Nontron and Jumilhac), Black Périgord (*Périgord Noir* — the south-east and Sarlat) and the Bergeracois (the south and south-west). These four regions are complemented by the forest lands, such as the Double and the Landais (west), and the rocky outcrops of the Quercy causses around Nadaillac, Daglan and Thenon. In this patchwork of landscapes with highly individual attractions, the unevenly spread population of some 380,000 inhabitants (over 500,000 in the 19th century) still has a marked rural character. Apart from a few significant industrial sectors, such as timber and wood by-products, leather, footwear and food processing, agriculture (crops and animal rearing) forms the main part of the region's activity. Indeed, Périgord is the nation's leading region for tobacco and strawberry production, and the second for walnuts and fat poultry.

Front cover:
on the bank of the Dordogne,
Beynac crowned by its castle.

Back cover:
Rue Montaigne, Sarlat.

Introduction

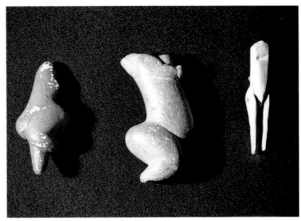

Underground Périgord
Prehistoric Périgord

Périgord possesses a number of **caves** open to the public which are all worth a visit; not only limestone caves, such as Domme and Le Grand Roc caves in Les Eyzies, and **chasms**, such as the one at Proumeyssac, near Le Bugue, but also the most famous prehistoric caves known to date (forty-eight in total). It is here, in this privileged land above all others, that evidence of prehistoric times is most concentrated. Indeed, the area has hundreds of sites, rock shelters and caverns where our distant ancestors left, voluntarily or otherwise, moving traces of their life on earth, tens of thousands of years before the Pyramids were built. And what traces! Facing the splendid paintings of the **Lascaux** vaults, Father Breuil, the "pope of prehistory", made a fitting comparison: "The Prehistoric Sistine Chapel". The original cave is closed to the public as the excessive numbers of visits were in danger of degrading this unique piece of heritage for ever. A few metres away, however, the famous friezes can be admired through a faithfully accurate, realistic "**fac-simile**".

Although Périgord cannot claim to be the birthplace of humanity (even if the remains of **Cro-Magnon man** were discovered here), it is in its valleys, along ochre cliffs towering above its rivers, that man created art. A number of sites in Black Périgord have given their name to cultural features which typify an epoch, such as **Mousterian** and **Magdalenian**, to mention but the most well-known. Quite naturally, this is also the place where prehistoric science was born and developed. The greatest prehistorians, Capitan, Peyrony, Leroi-Gourhan and Breuil, all worked here. In addition to Lascaux, Breuil listed two other caves in Les Eyzies among the six finest on the planet — **Font de Gaume** and **Les Combarelles**. If you are attracted by the engravings and paintings of horses, ibexes, reindeer and bison, then, hesitate no more. You should push on as far as Rouffignac and penetrate into the bowels of the earth to discover by train the miles of galleries in the **Grotte des Cent Mammouths** (the Cave of a Hundred Mammoths). This is but a summary of the extraordinary prehistoric wealth of the "**Land of Mankind**", the world's prehistoric capital, **Les Eyzies**, and the royal road, **listed "heritage of humanity"**, formed by the **Vézère valley**.

Les Eyzies museum: Prehistoric Venus stones.
In the centre: the Sireuil Venus *(9.2 x 5 cm).*
Lascaux II, in the main bull room:
bull (5.5 m) and red cow.

Near Montignac, Le Thot - reconstructed prehistoric habitat.

The bastide of Molières.

Hautefort, a castle from the age of Louis XIV lost in Périgord.

The mediaeval town of Sarlat. Stone roofs and Sainte-Marie church.

Historic Périgord

We know very little about our ancestors, the Petrocores. Along with other peoples, they took part in the resistance against Rome. Far more spectacular, being concentrated in two or three major sites, are the vestiges of the Gallo-Roman period — the gigantic **ruined tower** and arenas in Périgueux (formerly Vésone), fascinating **collections**, the results of numerous archaeological digs at the **Périgord museum**, significant **villa** remains in Montcaret and the Roman tower of La Rigale Castle in Villetoureix. It is highly probable that the first *cluzeaux*, artificial caves either above or below ground, date back to these times. These subterranean refuges and lookout huts could shelter entire populations. We have confirmation from Julius Caesar that the Gauls took refuge there. They can be found just about anywhere and very few cliffs have had no holes at all made in them.

Following the Barbarian invasions and the ephemeral Visigothic possession in the fifth century, Périgord became a part of the kingdom of Clovis after the battle of Vouillé and was subjected to the vicissitudes of its successors. This state of quasi-general confusion reached its crux during the repeated campaigns led by Pepin the Short against **Waïffre**, Duke of Aquitaine. Waïffre was finally to be killed, probably in the forests of La Double. Established as a county under Charlemagne, the whole region was pillaged by the **Vikings** for over a century from the 850's. Belonging for a while to the Angoumois region under Charles the Bald, Périgord was passed over, just a few years before the end of the first millennium, to the House of *La Marche* from which the **Talleyrands** descended, who themselves reigned for five centuries and provided several counts of Périgord. Our oldest seigneurial families appeared at this time — the Taillefers, the Birons, the Hauteforts, and so on. The independence of this nobility is perfectly characterised by Adalbert, Count of Périgord, of whom Hugues Capet enquired "Who made thou Count?", and who retorted "Who made thou King?".

Our first architectural masterpieces, however, date back to the eleventh and twelfth centuries, the period during which the feudal system gradually developed. Hundreds of **Romanesque churches** sprang up everywhere. Although the majority are quite humble, some bear a typical feature of Périgord, magnificent **pendentive-supported cupolas** (Saint-Front de Périgueux, Cherval, Trémolat...). The Ribérac area in particular has a number of splendid examples. We are now in a period of great awakening, change and expansion. The **troubadour's** art spread through Arnaud Daniel, Arnaud de Mareuil and particularly **Bertran de Born**. Romanesque sculptures and frescos embellish our churches and invite us in to pray (Besse, Cénac, Grand-Brassac...). Benedictine, Cistercian and Dominican priories and abbeys and Knight Templar commanderies provide evidence of the establishment of the Christian faith. Period of renewal, but also of uncertainty. Since the Guienne province had returned to the Crown under the Plantagenets following the remarriage of Eleanor of Aquitaine in 1152, Périgord passed by right under English suzerainty. In fact, being situated at the limit of the areas of influence of the two monarchies, it was to oscillate between the two dynasties for a long time. Over three hundred years of incessant struggle until 1453 and the end of the Hundred Years War were to tear apart and, as a consequence, model its physiognomy.

As at the time of the Norman invasions, the population took refuge in the cluzeaux and the numerous **cave forts**. The most famous sites, La Roque-Saint-Christophe and La Madeleine, were also inhabited from prehistoric times. Splendidly austere **fortified churches** (Saint-Amand-de-Coly, Tayac, Trémolat, Paunat…) thrust their towers with parapet walks, bartizans and battlements above the stone roofs of the houses huddled together in their protective shadow. Haughty, formidable **castles** reinforced the whole region. Beynac, Castelnaud and Commarque provide prestigious examples among many others. To the south and west, several fortified towns, known as *bastides*, sprang up from the 13th century, the majority being created by kings and counts. Population settlement centres and custodians of French and English charters, they were built according to a geometric plan around a central square. Domme, Monpazier and Beaumont have kept their mediaeval charm intact.

With the end of the Hundred Years War in 1453, the Castillon plain on the banks of the Dordogne, during the calmer periods of the late 15th and early 16th centuries, saw a development in **urban architecture**. The finest Gothic and Renaissance residences were built in Périgueux, Bergerac and Sarlat. In the countryside, the nobility had the majority of our **1200 châteaux**, manors and country houses erected.

In the second half of the sixteenth century, however, they experienced attacks, pillaging and fires as the Wars of Religion reached a rare degree of violence in Périgord. At the time, Bergerac was one of the most powerful Huguenot stongholds, along with La Rochelle. Following these wars, Périgord, fief of Henry of Navarre, was to return to the Crown for good and suffer henceforth from the sudden political changes of the French nation, from the Revolution to the tragic hours of the Resistance. We also encounter the memory of its most **illustrious literary figures**: Bertran de Born, Michel de Montaigne, Étienne de La Boëtie, Brantôme, Fénelon, Maine de Biran, Eugène Le Roy and André Maurois; its great captains: Talleyrand, Saint-Exupéry, Biron… and even Josephine Baker. A number of ruins (La Chapelle-Faucher, l'Herm…) have retained the memory of the tragedies which took place within their walls. Several of our castles and châteaux are open to visitors and some of them, such as Bourdeilles and Mareuil, house remarkable **collections**.

In addition to its castles, châteaux, churches, *bastides* and cave fortresses, Périgord has preserved from centuries past, a number of **wonderful villages** which still have their **market hall, dovecotes**, *bories* (stone huts), church, abbey and castle (s). Saint-Léon-sur-Vézère, Condat, Saint-Jean-de-Côle, La Roque-Gageac and many others are real jewels of architecture. As for the old quarters of Périgueux or Bergerac, restored and developed into pedestrian areas, they have regained their former charm. A number of small towns, such as Brantôme, Issigeac, Eymet and Mareuil, have withstood the often brash changes of modern times. A special mention should be made in this respect to Sarlat and Black Périgord.

"Cyrano" in Bergerac. Made famous by Edmond Rostand.

Brantôme: bronze bust of Pierre de Bourdeille, author of La Vie des Dames Galantes.

Cross of the "Knights Templars" in Sarlat.

Hunting for truffles.
Today, the locals search for the black diamond,
the Tuber melanosporum, *with dogs... and flies.*

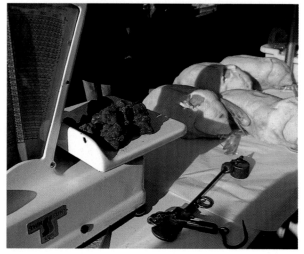

The foie gras and truffles stall.

The cep. Don't forget your basket!

Gastronomic Périgord

There are words which arouse more basic pleasures than castles, landscapes, churches or caves. There are terms which deliciously tantalise the taste buds of gourmands and gourmets alike. They go under the names are conserve of goose, truffled pâté, *magrets* of duck, cep mushroom omelette, stuffed neck, walnut cake..., enough to tempt even the most fanatical followers of calorie-controlled diets. Let's be honest about it, the cuisine of Périgord is ill-suited to such diets. It is rich, nourishing and based essentially on healthy farm produce. These rustic, tasty dishes represent the food of the land, which prestigious chefs have adapted to modern eating habits. Here, in Périgord, don't be surprised to see locals finish off their soup or "tourin" by pouring wine into their bowl, a practice known locally as "***faire chabrol***". Our gastronomy is, in fact, the result of a long country tradition.

You should taste *Mique* which the legendary revolutionary hero, *Jacquou le Croquant*, used to enjoy so much at Christmas; you should taste *pastis*, an apple cake which our neighbours from Quercy also make very well; you should taste the conserves of goose and duck, Sarlat potatoes, "Périgueux" sauce, partridge with morels... and sample the wines of the Bergerac region: Monbazillac and Pécharmant, the Montravel so appreciated by Montaigne, and the Saussignac praised by Rabelais. And not forgetting of course the **truffle**, our rare, highly sought black diamond, which... no, we'll stop and leave gourmets the indescribable pleasure of discovering for themselves the greatest masterpieces of this culinary art which, for many of our compatriots, goes hand in hand with a real art of living and the "**science of eating and drinking**".

The stone huts of Le Breuil, between Sarlat and Les Eyzies.

Périgord, now and forever

Having such a rich artistic background, it is not surprising that a special kind of tourism, which one might appropriately qualify as "cultural", has developed, as it is true that visitors do not come to Périgord by chance. But when even the caves and castles hold no more secrets for visitors, there will still be a thousand things for them to discover — megaliths, canoe trips down the river, walks through the forests, remote hamlets at points where, suddenly, the footpath is interrupted by a farmyard or a duck pond. They will still be able to wander through Gallic oppidums, "Caesar's camps" and down innumerable tracks led by their curiosity. Accommodation is offered by several hotels, camp sites, bed & breakfasts and farmhouse hostels which have been providing a **quality welcome** for around twenty years. The additional benefit of staying in a farmhouse is that it gives visitors the chance to experience a rural environment and perceive what constitutes the real wealth of Périgord — its people.

This is the real Périgord which we invite visitors to discover. If their taste for travel matches that of Montaigne, if they mark out "no particular paths, neither straight nor curved", if, like Périgord's most famous son, they give themselves the time to observe, and not just take a look, the time to smell and taste, then, and only then, will Périgord, like a beautiful woman, reveal all her charms. This is what wonderful Périgord is all about.

Brantôme.

A walnut sheller. The Dordogne is the second département in France for walnut production.

The cliff and the fort at Vitrac.

Between the Dordogne and the Vézère –
Black Périgord

Castelnaud: castle and village

Black Périgord, *whose capital is Sarlat,*
owes its name to the dark foliage of its green oaks and its vegetation in general.
*It offers visitors a variety of magical landscapes. This "**golden triangle**" marked out by the*
valleys of the Vézère, royal road of the prehistoric world, and the Dordogne with its
flamboyant châteaux, has retained its secretive yet welcoming appearance.

SARLAT

Sarlat, the geographical centre of Périgord-Quercy, is by far the most **important tourist site** in the region. Over a million visitors discover or rediscover this **mediaeval jewel** every year. This town of 10,000 inhabitants today occupies top spot in terms of tourists and culture. Although this is basically a cultural town, industry is also represented, mainly by food processing firms, many of which produce *foie gras*. This foie gras, one of the most highly rated in France, has contributed to the great culinary reputation of Périgord in general and the town in particular.

Although it has one of the largest **mediaeval urban areas** (13th to 16th centuries) in the world, Sarlat cannot claim a very distant past. The initial Sarlat abbey was most probably founded between 820 and 840 by Duke Pepin of Aquitaine. **Saint Bernard** stopped off in Sarlat in 1147 during his journey throughout the South of France to spread the Gospel to the many Cathars. The plague was predominant at the time. He gave the sick consecrated bread to eat and healed them. This event, this miracle even, was commemorated by the building of the strange **graveyard lantern** which, still today, remains one of the town's symbols. The town, which had grown in the shadow of its religious community, gradually obtained its autonomy marked by the suppression of taxation in 1204 and the **election of consuls** from 1223.

The salamander on Sarlat's coat of arms.

Stone roofs in Sarlat.

The house of La Boëtie.
Étienne de La Boëtie was born here in 1530.
Right: Étienne de La Boëtie. Humanist thinker
and intimate friend of Michel de Montaigne.

Forerunners to our municipal council, the four consuls and the eighty jurats governed the town and enjoyed legal powers. In 1317, Pope John XXII from Quercy created the **bishopric** of Sarlat, henceforth separated from the diocese of Périgueux. During the Hundred Years War, Sarlat was never taken by the English in spite of the plague which ravaged the ranks of the defenders. Donadei, the traitor, who plotted to give up the town square, was **stitched up in a sack** and **thrown into the Cuze**. The treaty of Brétigny (1360) surrendered the town to the English and the famous captain, John Chandos, received the keys. When fighting started up again in 1370, prompted by Du Guesclin who had returned to re-awaken the warrior spirit amongst the bourgeois, Sarlat rallied the lilied banner of Charles V. From 1404, the Sarlat troops played an active part in the reconquest of Périgord right up until the final victory. A victory which was dearly paid for as the diocese was left in ruins. Half of the town's residences were rebuilt between 1450 and 1500 in an early **Renaissance** style. The majority of the town's architectural masterpieces date back to this period.

Appointed bishop in 1492, **Armand de Gontaut-Biron** undertook the task of completing Sainte-Marie church, begun in 1368. In 1533, a new bishop, a relation of Catherine de Medici, the Florentine **Nicolas Gaddi**, had the Episcopal palace built next to the cathedral according to the fashion in Italy. In spite of a new plague epidemic in 1521-22, claiming 3000 lives, the middle of the 16th century saw a healthy cultural life develop in

Sarlat. The **humanism** of the Renaissance period did not prevent religious fanaticism from breaking out. In 1562, Duras laid siege to the town which was freed by a Royal army. In 1574, for the first time in the town's history, Sarlat was taken by military force by **Geoffroy de Vivans** who dispersed the relics of Saint Sacerdos, before he too was chased off.

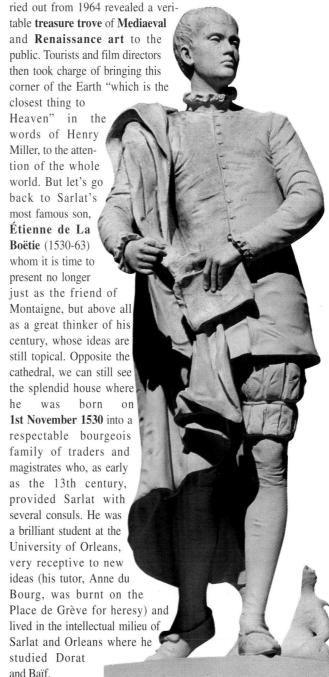

Lost in the heart of distant Périgord, Sarlat could have sunk into oblivion if it was not for the **Malraux Act** of 4th August 1962. Perhaps the Minister of Culture recalled having taken to the *maquis*, in the heart of the Sarlat woodlands, when he signed the act on **renovation** and **restoration**. The works carried out from 1964 revealed a veritable **treasure trove** of **Mediaeval** and **Renaissance art** to the public. Tourists and film directors then took charge of bringing this corner of the Earth "which is the closest thing to Heaven" in the words of Henry Miller, to the attention of the whole world. But let's go back to Sarlat's most famous son, **Étienne de La Boëtie** (1530-63) whom it is time to present no longer just as the friend of Montaigne, but above all as a great thinker of his century, whose ideas are still topical. Opposite the cathedral, we can still see the splendid house where he was born on **1st November 1530** into a respectable bourgeois family of traders and magistrates who, as early as the 13th century, provided Sarlat with several consuls. He was a brilliant student at the University of Orleans, very receptive to new ideas (his tutor, Anne du Bourg, was burnt on the Place de Grève for heresy) and lived in the intellectual milieu of Sarlat and Orleans where he studied Dorat and Baïf.

It was at this time that he wrote his *Discours sur la servitude volontaire*. This red hot text which tasted strongly of heresy was circulated in secret and was only published after his death by Protestants. La Boëtie also wrote a number of **poems** including a famous sonnet dedicated to the river Dordogne. At 23 years of age, he entered the Bordeaux parliament as an alderman, then married a young widow, Marguerite de Carle. In 1558, he met **Montaigne**, his junior by three years, who already held him in high esteem ("We were searching for each other before we saw each other") and who always to consider him as his master of thought ("He surpassed me by an infinite distance"). Their exemplary **friendship** lasted for six years and is summed up by these now famous words, extracted from Montaigne's *Essais*: "If one were to press me to say why I loved him, I know that this may only be expressed by answering '**because it was he and because it was I**'". In June 1563, the plague broke out in Sarlat. La Boëtie fell ill in Germinian, at the home of Montaigne's brother-in-law. He died on 18th August 1563, attended by his friend to whom he left his book collection and his precious manuscripts.

We shall begin our visit to the mediaeval town by the **Place de la Grande-Rigaudie**, in the centre of which Étienne de La Boëtie, fixed in stone, observes undauntedly the crowd of visitors. By taking Rue de Tourny (formerly the main street), we reach the **Place du Peyrou** where Saint-Sacerdos cathedral stands proud. Just before the square, you will notice, on the left, on the corner of Rue Bonnel, a fine 18th century façade and, on the right, the **Episcopal palace**, with its double transom windows, built by bishop Nicolas Gaddi. This rather austere building whose façade is decorated with **sculptures** of telamones, heads and monsters, was crowned in the 20th century by an elegant "Italian" gallery. Three listed residences face the entrance to the cathedral — one is a 16th century half-timbered house, another is a former 18th century inn. The third, which you will have noticed immediately, is the symbol of the town — the superb **house of La Boëtie**. The highly ornate façade is a masterpiece of Italian influenced Renaissance architecture. Its sculpted transom windows are framed by medallions and pilasters and surmounted by ornate gable windows and tall chimneys. On the outside, you will notice the stone roofing, the sculpted gable ends and **sheep**, the La Boëtie family arms, on the walls (see the 16th century **Château de la Boëtie** on the Vitrac road out of Sarlat).

Saint-Sacerdos cathedral, a former Benedictine abbey church, became a see in 1317. Of the Romanesque building, which itself succeeded a Carolingian construction, there remains a **porch-belfry** whose portal, redesigned in the 17th century, is surmounted by **five statues** of mysterious origin (one of them is said to represent Atlas carrying the globe) and which are very difficult to date. Of the three storeys of the belfry topped by a bulb roof, dating back to the 18th century, the first is decorated with tall blind arcades while the following two have bays.

Facing page: Place du Peyrou and the house of La Boëtie.

The apse of Saint-Sacerdos cathedral.

Work was carried out on the church from 1318 to 1790. The main part of the **edifice** dates back to the **16th century** — the vast nave with its four bays, side-aisles and ribbed vaults supported by massive pillars. It ends in a five-sided chancel surrounded by an ambulatory and a more ancient apse. The **rich furnishings** include several carved retables, a pulpit decorated with the tetramorph, 18th century stalls, and an 18th century gallery which supports authentic **Lépine organs**, amongst the finest in France, the force of which makes the old walls vibrate during concerts. The vestry, with its ribbed vaults, is the former 14th century chapter-house. Leaving via the southern aisle and passing round the side of the church, we discover the small chapel of the *Pénitents bleus* (Blue Penitents), also known as Saint-Benoît's chapel, the interior of which has a very pure Romanesque style. Let's cross the Cour des Fontaines and the Cour des Chanoines, surrounded by beautiful houses. Through an opening in the form of an arc of a circle, hidden in the corner of a wall, we reach the *jardin des pénitents* (the Garden of the Penitents, also known as the *jardin des enfeus* — the garden of recesses). The former town cemetery, the terraces of which are decorated with antique tombstones, is overlooked on one side by the cathedral and, on the other, by the strange silhouette of the **graveyard lantern**. This is a charmingly peaceful place which, in summer, acts as a venue for concerts and plays. Continuing round the apse, we discover the **recesses**, stone niches which contained the sarcophagi of eminent people of Sarlat. Access to the graveyard lantern can be gained by a flight of steps. The usage of this mysterious 12th century building, in the form of a shell or a rocket, is unknown.

Crossing the steep Rue Montaigne, lined with old houses, we reach the narrow **Rue d'Albusse** where a vast triple building (n° 2-4) housed the escapades of **General Fournier-Sarlovèze**. At the end of the road, in Rue Salamandre which leads down towards the heart of the town, at n° 1, **Grézel House** raises its polygonal tower, which features a 15th century portal, decorated with a salamander - the fabulous beast which appears on the town's coat of arms. Above Grézel House, at n° 6, Rue du Présidial, the 15th century **Genis (or Beaupuy) House**, which was subsequently altered in the 18th century, shows off a porch with pilasters, crowned by a triangular pediment, and a gallery topped by a porch roof. To the right, in Rue Landry, standing before a splendid garden is one of the town's finest buildings — the **Présidial**, the former **courthouse**, established by Henry II in

Facing page: The graveyard lantern, also known as the Lantern of the Moors. Its name and style could have been brought back from the Holy Land by the Knights Templars.

A house in Rue Montaigne, near the graveyard lantern.

The recesses, stone niches containing the sarcophagi of eminent people of Sarlat.

The "Présidial", seat of the former courthouse established by Henry II.

1552 and which, in the 17th century, accommodated up to ten prosecutors and thirteen barristers.

With its two vast loggias, its façade covered in Virginia creepers and its strange **roof turret**, it is certainly an attractve building. At the end of Rue du Présidial, lined with various residences built into the ramparts, we reach Rue Fénelon.

To the left, preceded by a 16th century house, we find, at n° 16, **Salignac house**, dating back to the 15th and 18th centuries, where the aunts of Fénelon lived. It features a gargoyle and, to the rear, a Gothic window. Opposite, at n° 13, stands the splendid Aillac House (16th century), with its polygonal tower, Renaissance windows and pointed chimney. This building, which was a convent in the 17th century, today houses the **Musée des Mirepoises** (arms, armour, furniture, etc.). Proceeding down the street, four 15th century residences with Renaissance windows can be admired at n°s 8, 10, 12 and 14, while n° 6 features a 17th century portal. At n° 3, at the back of a courtyard, **Gérard** (or Du Barry) **House**, which dates back to the 14th and 18th centuries, was once one of the town's finest but is now largely dilapidated. The vast building still has a columned gallery, a pedimented portal and a Gothic win-dow. At the bottom of Rue Fénelon, at n° 1, a fine rounded building dating back to the 17th century, with an open ground floor complete with arcades and with sculpted gable windows, conceals in its back yard the tower of a **15th century house**, with a Gothic porch decorated with sculptures of distinguished people.

On the Place de la Liberté in the centre of Sarlat, the splendid **town hall** built in 1615 by the Monpazier architect, Henri Bouyssou, features, on the ground floor, covered arcades and, on the first floor, a balustraded balcony crowned by a frieze. A pinnacle turret emerges from the roof. The magnificent **Place de la Liberté** (ex-Place Royale), bordered on all sides by old houses, ventilated with arcades, is a great picture of harmony. It acts as a setting for a drama festival and has inspired almost all of the film directors who have come to shoot in Black Périgord, including Jacques Ertaud for *Sans Famille*, Frank Roddam for *La Promise* and Robert Hossein who set up the gallows for *Les Misérables* here. Waiting to be discovered opposite the town hall are an arcaded house with an 18th century façade at n°s 5 and 6 and the splendid **Vienne** (or Maleville) House with a double façade, at n° 7, where Jean de Vienne, financial secretary under Henry IV, and later the descendants of the jurist, Jacques de Maleville, lived.

This true little château has a square turret staircase, set back, and a Renaissance portal, the spandrel of which is decorated with medallions representing Henry IV and Gabrielle d'Estrée (or Marie de Medici). On either side, the house, which features a bartizan, has transom windows. On the square, a former shop, surmounted with three remarkable **Renaissance windows**, houses the tourist information centre. The interior conceals a French-style ceiling and a painted, sculpted fireplace depicting a deer between two hounds. Beneath the building, a side street disappears into a covered alley. Opposite Vienne House, at n° 5, the 14th century Dautrerie House has an old shop on the ground floor and, at the crest of the gable, the sculpture of a leopard. The entrance, hidden in a cul-de-sac, leads to a magnificent Renaissance staircase. The square extends into **Rue de la Liberté**, lined with old façades, which provides a view of the cathedral belfry. On the right, you will see a round-towered pharmacy, followed by three half-timbered houses (n°s 2, 4 and 8). A side street reveals the sculpted Gothic porch, closed by a magnificent studded door, of La Mothe House.

Heading off to the right, behind La Boëtie's house, we enter a network of **small courtyards** separated by vaulted passageways

On the Place de la Liberté:
Sarlat is turned into Budapest for the filming of "La Promise" (1984).

Place de la Liberté: the Saturday market.

Vienne house. Jean de Vienne,
financial secretary under Henry IV, lived here.

The 16th century Chassaing house. This château, in the heart of the
old town, provides a splendid natural setting to the Drama Festival.

Facing page: Vassal House, on the small goose-market square.

— a perfect example of what urbanism may have been in the Middle Ages. This is a maze of half-timbered houses, overhangs and turrets; you might be forgiven for thinking that you are about to be caught in a cul-de-sac at any moment, but the alley slips through a little gateway and carries on. Continuing down **Rue Albéric-Cahuet**, which reveals further antique residences, past the old hospital and the rear of Vienne House, we reach **Sainte-Marie church**, built from 1368 to 1479, of which we caught a glimpse as we crossed the Place de la Liberté. The building was damaged, and the destroyed apse has been replaced by a stained glass window. Two bays of the nave, roofed in stone, remain in addition to the side chapels and a decapitated belfry, with a warlike appearance, which is decorated with statues and monstrous **gargoyles**. A covered market and a panoramic elevator are to take their place. Continuing round to the right of the church, we discover the opu-

lent 16th century **Chassaing House** (also owned later by Magnanat, and then Gisson) which, in fact, consists of two houses joined by a hexagonal turret staircase and which provides a splendid natural setting to the Drama Festival. One of the houses features, side by side, a triple Gothic window with colonnettes and a Renaissance transom bay. Beyond this residence, **Rue Magnanat** rises up to the house of the **Royal Notary**, with its remarkable 17th century portal, and then descends once again, revealing yet more interesting porches as we go by. The former main thoroughfare, **Rue des Consuls**, where the residences of the eminent people of Sarlat were gathered, begins at the other side of the church. On the right, at n° 9, on the tiny goose-market square, the 15th century **Vassal House** is perhaps the most picturesque in the town with its double bartizan which joins the two houses at right angles and its transom windows. N° 14 is where we find the 17th century

Labrousse House. Further on, to the left, at n°s 8-10, we reach the most famous of the Sarlat mansions, **Plamon House**, built by this grand consular family of drapers, ennobled in the 14th century. This building is to accommodate the **Musée du Sarladais** (history, geography, art and popular traditions). Its architecture has remained harmonious in spite of the variety of styles added by successive periods. The ground and first floors opens out through **14th century pointed arches**, true lacework in stone, whereas the second floor has 15th century transom bays. The porch and the staircase date back to the 17th century. A variety of **sculptures** of hounds and people, some of which are obscene, may be noticed on the façade, in addition to a number of hooks for suspending banners and tapestries on feast days. Opposite are situated the fresh **Sainte-Marie's fountain** with its ribbed vaults and the 15th century **Mirandol House** with its pedimented porch. At the corner of the street, at right angles, a fine stone pendentive, crowned with a balcony and forged iron railings allowed coaches to negotiate the corner of the street. At n° 6, the 15th century **Tapinois de Betou House** features a remarkable 17th century wooden staircase. Beyond there, Rue des Consuls rejoins the main road.

Before visiting the western sector of the town, you might wish to catch a glimpse of this main road, Rue de la République, known as *La Traverse* ("the Crossing") by the locals, driven right into the heart of the old quarters between 1837 and 1840.

Rue des Armes, which begins opposite Rue des Consuls, seems to be blocked by a splendid 15th century ribbed, **half-timbered residence**. At n° 2, the façade of the house of Ravilhon, again from the 15th century, features pointed arch transom windows. Another 15th century residence spans the street which passes in front of the guardhouse before continuing up to the remains of the northern gate (the Turenne breach) and the ramparts. Via Rue de la Charité, we reach **Rue Jean-Jacques-Rousseau** by passing in front of the **Chapel of the Pénitents-Blancs**, with its monumental 17th century portal with pediment and columns, which houses the **Museum of Sacred Art**. It used to form part of **Les Récollets convent**, built between 1615 and 1628. Beyond the house of Monméja with its 17th century façade, at n° 9, we discover the vast 17th century **Sainte-Claire's convent** and its bartizan. This former Clarisses' convent which was used as a prison during the Revolution, then as a hospice, was restored by the *Club du Vieux Manoir*. Having left behind the picturesque **Côte de Toulouse**, where venerable houses are built one below another down the steep road, we turn left into **Rue de La Boëtie** to discover, at n° 9, the 15th century **Maynard House** which features ogival windows, transom bays, and a splendid walnut staircase. The end of the street loses itself in a maze of alleys. Let's go back up via the narrow **Rue Rousset** where we find the 15th century **Saint-Clar** House and its round machicolated **watchtower**. This building, which is a real little château with its Renaissance bays, also has a bartizan. At the top of the hill, we shall bear left into **Rue du Siège** which offers a succession of ancient houses — residences from the 15th century at n° 5, the 14th century with its Gothic windows at n° 8 and, at the corner of Rue des Trois-Conils, the 17th century **Cerval House**. The right-hand side of the street skirts the ramparts (visible from Rue de Turenne), which contains a gateway and is surmounted by the **Tour du Bourreau**. Before reaching *La Traverse*, we shall need to go back up Rue du Barry and take **Rue des Trois-Conils** on the right. The old residence which we discover, with its 15th century tower concealing a spiral staircase, is the **Marzac House**. Madeleine-Marie de Bart, daughter of Jean Bart and wife of Seigneur de Vérignac, died in this house in 1791. Rue de Trois-Conils which disappears beneath a covered passage with askew windows, leads to **Place Liarsou** in front of a superb **half-timbered house** with balcony where the Boyt de Mérignac family, related to the La Boëties, lived. To the left, **Rue de Cordil** reveals the other façade of Saint-Clar House with its Renaissance windows. To the right, Rue La Boëtie, which crosses the main street, brings you back to the foot of the cathedral.

Above the Place de la Grande-Rigaudie, the **Jardin du Plantier**, drawn by Le Nôtre at the request of Fénelon, brings an air of freshness to the town centre and offers a pleasant view of the roofs of Sarlat. To the north, by the former hospital, a fine 18th century building, the **cultural centre** hosts plays, concerts and exhibitions. Nearby, on Rue du Commandant-Maratuel, the **Aquarium Museum** is home for around a hundred fish (trout, pike, salmon, sturgeon, etc.). To the south, on Avenue Thiers, the **Motor Vehicle Museum** houses a splendid collection.

Sarlat is buzzing with cultural activity, particularly in the summer months, centred around the **Festival des Jeux du Théâtre** (Drama festival), created in 1962, prompted by J. Boisserie. This festival, the first in Aquitaine and the oldest in France after

Facing page: Plamon house and its 14th century pointed arches.

Old street: the work of art and the model.

Avignon, is one of the nation's seven or eight major festivals. Sarlat has seen some of the leading lights of the Comédie Française and other prestigious troupes, such as the Théâtre du Campagnol (*Le Bal*), the Magic Circus by J. Savary and Robert Hossein (*Les Loups by R. Rolland*). The main settings for the **music festival**, which provides a number of high quality concerts, are the cathedral and the cultural centre, while the former bishopric acts as venue for the national exhibition of **photographic art**. But one of the most unusual aspects of the cultural scene in Sarlat is the place held by the film industry, which has seen the creation of an **audiovisual festival** (in November) on the theme of the art of living. Indeed, with over thirty films shot in the capital of Black Périgord, Sarlat and the surrounding area have become the **third centre for filming** in France, after Paris and Nice. Above Sarlat, a pilgrimage to the virgin of **Temniac**, who lives in a beautiful Romanesque chapel, is a must. Open to visitors, the castle, traditionally founded by the Knights Templars, was the property of the bishops of Sarlat.

Temniac church conceals a miraculous Virgin in its crypt.

SALIGNAC and EYRIGNAC
(17 km N.E. of Sarlat)

Curiously situated below the village, the imposing **Salignac Castle** is **open to visitors**. This is one of the oldest fortified places in the region. Indeed, there is evidence of its existence as early as the 11th century and it was rebuilt in the 12th and 13th centuries. A large part of the present-day buildings were constructed in the 15th and 17th centuries. This antique fortress of the **Salignac de la Mothe-Fénelon** family, ancestors of the Archbishop of Cambrai, played an important role during the Hundred Years War and the Wars of Religion. In 1545, residence of the austere citadel passed to the Gontaut-Birons who transformed it into a Renaissance house. Still surrounded by ramparts, the 15th century two-storey upper part of the building, roofed in stone and featuring transom windows, stand next to two round

Salignac Castle. Fief of the Salignac de la Mothe-Fénelon family, ancestors of the great writer Fénelon.

The ornamental gardens of Eyrignac Manor.

The South of Black Périgord: The Dordogne Valley

SAINTE-MODANE FÉNELON

(17 km S.E. of Sarlat)

Lost in the mists of the Middle Ages, the origins of the village of Sainte-Modane combines history and legend. In the eighth century, the Governor of Aquitaine, Amicius, gave **Laban** and his wife, **Mondane**, the charge of commanding the Sarlat region. They founded Calviac Abbey and their son, **Saint Sacerdos**, became Bishop of Limoges and patron saint of Sarlat.

Above the village and overlooking the Dordogne and the **Bouriane** woods, **Fénelon Castle** is **open to visitors**. Built in the 15th century, it pleasantly combines the warlike character of the Middle Ages and the aesthetics of the Renaissance period. The castle includes, to the south, a Renaissance house, framed by two circular towers, and whose gable windows have sculpted pediments; to the east, a square 15th century pavilion and two round towers from the 14th and 15th centuries, one of which contains the oratory where Fénelon prayed. The west wing combines mediaeval and Renaissance parts. It is joined to the main house by a round turret staircase. A very deep well is to be found nearby. To the north, a 17th century balcony and a terrace decorated with a balustrade. Access is gained to the main courtyard via a double **staircase** and a drawbridge.

towers, crowned with watch turrets, and a rectangular dungeon with close buttresses.

Inside the arms room and the main drawing room, we shall discover splendid 15th and 16th century fireplaces, Renaissance furniture, a portrait of Fénelon and Flemish tapestries. We can still see two storeys of cellars and the remains of a Romanesque chapel which bear the traces of frescos. Nearby, we shall be able to visit the remarkable **gardens** of **Eyrignac Manor**. Created in the 18th century, they have been restored to their original level of ornamental perfection.

Overleaf: The "Cingle de Montfort" at dawn. The fortress of the Cathar, Bernard de Casnac, has been rebuilt several times.

Fénelon Castle. François Salignac de la Mothe-Fénelon was born here in 1651.

Our visit leads us to discover many things, not least of which the attic with its strong chestnut timber work which supports the impressive weight of the **stone** roof (almost one tonne per square metre), and the **bedroom** of **François Salignac de la Mothe-Fénelon**, who was born within these walls on 6th August 1651.

In the 17th century, following the death of his first wife who had already given him eleven children, **Pons de Salignac** married **Louise de La Cropte-Chantérac** who gave birth to the illustrious **writer**. After a childhood spent at the castle, he began studying at the University of Cahors in 1663 under the aegis of his uncle, the Bishop of Sarlat. He continued his education in Paris until 1672. Having entered the seminary, he was ordained **priest** around 1675. Abandoning his missionary vocation for health reasons, he firstly became priest of **Carennac**, in the Lot, before directing the convent of the "New Catholics" from 1678 to 1689. He drew on this experience to write his *Traité sur l'éducation des filles*. In 1689, he became preceptor to the Duke of Burgundy, grandson of Louis XIV, for whom he wrote his *Fables*, the *Dialogues des Morts* and *Télémaque*, his main work, written from 1694 to 1696. He was elected to the Académie Française on 7th March 1693 and was appointed Archbishop of Cambrai on 4th February 1695. The period from 1697 to 1699 was marked by the famous jousts between **Bossuet,** *the Meaux Eagle*, and Fénelon, *the Cambrai Swan*. Defender of "**quietism**", so dear to Madame Guyon, a mystical stance in which Bossuet saw the danger of heresy, Fénelon was vanquished by his redoubtable opponent, disgraced by the king and exiled in 1699 to his archbishopric in Cambrai where he passed away on 1st January 1715, at the age of 63. Although far from his place of birth, Fénelon embellished his work with Périgord landscapes and portraits. In *Télémaque*, many a reader has taken pleasure in recognising Sarlat in *Salente*, the ideal city of the sage Mentor. In particular, he denounces royal absolutism, condemns the adverse effects of war and preaches a return to rustic morals and a healthy life in this work. He may be considered, at the dawn of the Age of Enlightenment, to have been the precursor to Montesquieu, Voltaire and Rousseau. The "philosophers" took inspiration from some of his ideas. Indeed, it is difficult not to be struck by the revolutionary tones of Fénelon: "**Kings are made for their subjects and not the subjects for their kings**". Moreover, Rousseau made no mistake when he paid this fine tribute to him: "If Fénelon were alive, I should seek to be his footman in order to become his valet". Nearby, you should also pay a visit to **Veyrignac** castle (museum, balloon rides). See also **Carlux** Fortress, **Rouffillac** Castle (15th and 17th centuries) and the splendid ruins of **Paluel** Castle (14th and 15th centuries).

The ruins of Paluel Castle.

MONTFORT
(8 km south of Sarlat)

If you do not have the chance to take a boat ride along the river, you will at least be able to discover Montfort Castle from the **panoramic view** of the "**cingle de Montfort**", on the road from Carsac, at the point where a meander in the River Dordogne — the "cingle" — loops around Turnac peninsula. In the distance, the white cliffs of **Caudon** can be made out. Hanging over the cliff, as if it were suspended in the air, Montfort seems to be straight out of a fairy tale. The supporting cliff is perforated with caves which makes you wonder how the castle has managed not to be washed away with the waters like the legendary town of Ys. The ancient houses of this tiny village huddle around the foot of their powerful guardian.

The history of this castle (open to visitors) is marked by its relentless fight for survival. The fate of Montfort is somewhat strange and tumultuous as it was besieged and destroyed in 1214, 1309, 1350, 1481 and 1606 and rebuilt each time. The castle which we admire today is the result of eight centuries of construction work. In the early 13th century, it was the property of the cruel Catharist seigneur **Bernard de Casnac** and his wife, Alix de Turenne, who mutilated all Catholics who fell into their hands.

Men had their feet and hands chopped off and their eyes poked out; women had their breasts and their thumbs cut off. In 1214, during the crusade against the Albigensians, the formidable **Simon de Montfort** (his name is but a homonymy) sent troops to seize the castle. According to legend, Bernard's daughter, Blanche, was burnt alive and her ghost is said to haunt the fortress still today. See the beautiful sculpted Romanesque church in **Carsac**.

DOMME
(12 km south of Sarlat)

Constructed on a plateau overlooking the Dordogne valley, the **acropolis of Domme**, a town built for war, is an architectural and aesthetic masterpiece. This spot combines this exceptional site with the extraordinary **unity of style** of its old white stone houses with their brown tile roofs and flowery balconies.

In the early 13th century, the present-day town had still not been built, but, in its place, stood a **castle**, Domme-Vieille. In order to contain the advance of the English army, King Philip III (also known as Philip the Rash), recognising the strategic importance of the site, bought a part of the plateau in 1280 to found the *bastide* of Mont-de-Domme there. From 1280 to 1310, a number of difficul-

Montfort Castle - the result of eight centuries of construction work.

Domme, French bastide from the late 18th century - general view.

Facing page, top: Domme, "Porte del Bos".
Bottom: "Porte des Tours", one of the oldest gates in France. Its walls were used as a prison for the Knights Templars from 1307 to 1318.

ties were experienced in the construction of the town: access was difficult, the population very poor and the workmen were only paid in leather money struck in Domme — the obsidional.

Thereafter, the town retained the privilege of striking coins. Little by little, **the finest French *bastide* in Périgord** was raised in Domme.

Remarkable unity of style:
central market hall and governor's house.

In 1346, the English took possession through an act of treachery — some of the inhabitants opened the town's gates to them. In the following year, the Seneschal of Périgord liberated the town and had the traitors hung. In 1348, Philip VI granted a charter which guaranteed the autonomy of the city. The Hundred Years War was to see Domme swing from one side to the other. The English laid siege in 1369 and took it in 1393. The French in turn laid siege in 1421.

Following more than a century of peace, the Wars of Religion were to bring Domme back to the forefront. In 1572, the Huguenot captain, **Geoffroy de Vivans**, failed twice to take Domme. Neither siege nor treachery could open the city gates to him. He was even injured here. On 25th October 1588, a most foolhardy exploit finally enabled him to fulfil his ambition. Captain Bordes and Captain Bramarigues, escorted by thirty men, climbed, at nightfall, the cliffs of the "Barre de Domme" which, considered impregnable, were not defended. Once inside the citadel, they opened the doors and Vivans took possession of the town. In 1741, Domme was the birthplace of the jurist **Jacques de Maleville** who was one of the writers of French Common Law.

We might begin our visit of Domme by a tour of the ramparts. The early 14th century wall with a number of redans runs for

Knight Templar carvings in the "Porte des Tours".

several hundred metres. It has three gateways — the fortified **Porte del Bos**, formerly portcullised, the **Porte de la Combe** which leads down to a fountain, and the remarkable **Porte des Tours**, the finest fortified gateway in Périgord, built in the late 13th century.

Formerly protected by a drawbridge and a portcullis, it is defended by two enormous round half-towers which were used as watch towers and, from 1307 to 1318, as a prison for the **Knight Templars** of Périgord. Their drawings and inscriptions can still be seen on the walls.

Let's begin our visit of the town in Rue Eugène-Le Roy in which we discover the house of the writer. This leads us to **Place de la Rode**, meaning "wheel", where the execution of criminals took place. It features four splendid houses, including the house of the minter with its triple windows. The main street (Grand-Rue) is lined with houses with noble façades, ribbed vaults and ancient doors. At the corner of Rue Geoffroy-de-Vivans, we see a sculpted window dating back to the Renaissance period. In Rue des Consuls, the former town hall has a 13th century façade crowned by a tower. On **Place de la Halle**, the heart of the town, stands the 15th and 16th century **Governor's house**, flanked by its bartizan. The 17th century market hall conceals the entrance to the cave, the **Grotte du Jubilé, open to visitors**. Four hundred and fifty metres long, this cave reveals a entrancing world of white stalactites and stalagmites. The bison and mammoth bones displayed at the site were discovered during the excavation of the way in. A **panoramic elevator** takes visitors up the side of the cliff. The Paul-Reclus **museum** is devoted to the discoveries made in Domme and particularly to prehistoric times. Continuing past the parish church with its wall-belfry, we discover the "**Barre de Domme**" — a sheer 150 metre drop over the meandering river Dordogne and its rich, cultivated plain, the most famous **panorama** in Périgord.

If there are places in the world which seem to increase the creative capacity of writers, then Domme is one of these "hills of inspiration". It dictated to **Henry Miller**, who visited the town before the war, the introduction to one of his most well-known works, *The Colossus of Marousi*. Listen to him speaking of Périgord from the top of the "Barre de Domme", hear this fine plea for our land: "This is a land of enchantment jealously marked by poets and which they alone have the right to call their own. Which is closest to heaven… Nothing will stop me believing that if Cro-Magnon man settled here, it was because he was extremely intelligent and had a highly developed sense of beauty… Nothing will stop me believing that this great, peaceful region of France is destined to remain a sacred place for man and that, when the big city has finished wiping out poets, their successors will find refuge and a birthplace here… **It is possible that one day France will cease to be, but Périgord will survive like the dreams which nourish the human soul**". At the bottom of Domme, **Cénac** church features a 12th century sculpted apse.

The tiny 14th century church in the village of La Roque-Cageac.

The cliff at La Roque-Gageac, an exceptional site for an exceptional village.

LA ROQUE-GAGEAC
(12 km south of Sarlat)

The **third site in France**, after Mont-Saint-Michel and Rocamadour, La Roque-Gageac was awarded, a few years ago, the envied title of the "most beautiful village in France". At the foot of a steep **cliff** crowned with green oaks, castles and residences, remarkably **united** in tone and style, snuggle up against the rocky bluff as if they were trying to blend better into the majestic landscape and admire themselves in the green waters of the Dordogne. The houses with their brown tile roofs seem to be cut from the white mass of the high cliff. Depending on the course of the sun and the time of day, all variations of ochre, white and grey transform the village and its aquatic reflection into a veritable riot of iridescent colours.

In the Middle Ages, this was in fact a prosperous, **free** little town of 1500 inhabitants, governed by two consuls, where the Bishops of Sarlat had their country residence. La Roque-Gageac was also an active port, trading in timber, wine, iron, salt and all sorts of food produce.

To appreciate the full charm of the village, you need to wander through the narrow streets which seem to run along the rooftops. You will discover a pretty 14th century church with its wall-belfry and an apse which extends the rock on which it stands, and charming houses typical of Périgord, surrounded by stunning **Mediterranean vegetation**, favoured by the micro-climate created by the sun on heating the rock. As you climb up the slopes, you will enjoy the beautiful **panorama** over the valley. You will also be able to visit the cave fort, dug into the side of the cliff, which acted as a base for the bishops' castle.

Downstream, almost at road level, the **Château de la Malartrie**, in spite of its 20th century neo-Gothic style, does not stand out in this mediaeval decor.

One family from La Roque-Gageac dominates local history — the **Tarde** family. We still have not mentioned their **manor**, with its elegant round, stone-roofed tower which stands alongside two gabled main buildings containing transom windows. If you had been walking, as a bourgeois or country bumpkin, one night, around the year 1615, somewhere near the château, you might have noticed a strange instrument with an elongated shape, pointed in the direction of Orion or Andromeda. You would undoubtedly have bowed to the illustrious canon bent over the eye-piece. Indeed, **Jean Tarde**, who was born in La Roque-Gageac in 1561 and who died in the same village 75 years later, brought the first astronomical telescope in Périgord, and one of the first in the whole of France, back from his second journey to Italy where it was handed to him by his friend, **Galileo Galilei**. You should know that Jean Tarde, at the time, was as famous as his elder, Pico della Mirandola, and if history has forgotten Jean Tarde, it is because our canon, humanist, astronomer, numismatist, geographer, theologian, philosopher and historian preferred the solitude of his manor and the decor of his Black Périgord to the crowds and marble halls of palatial houses.

Facing page: La Roque-Gageac, Château de la Malartrie.
Its neo-Gothic style slots perfectly into the village setting.

Above a sea of mist, Beynac Castle - the "King of Périgord".

BEYNAC
(10 km S.W. of Sarlat)

The **site** of Beynac and its castle is undoubtedly one of the finest in France. The village where **Paul Eluard** was born is built in stages above the water's edge, at the bottom of a 150 metre **cliff topped** by an impressive **fort**. This eagle's nest might seem rather austere if it were not for the sun lighting up its golden walls, mirrored by the Dordogne. With its changing colours and the luminosity of the stone, the sky and the water, Beynac is a paradise for painters and photographers in all seasons.

Following the organisation of the county of Périgord, it became the seat of one of the four **baronies** along with Biron, Bourdeilles and Mareuil. The first unquestionable trace of a seigneur of Beynac dates back to 1115. The castle was so powerful and its barons so cruel that local vassals and peasants named it "**Satan's ark**".

In 1214, on return from a crusade against the Albigensians, Simon de Montfort took possession of Beynac, whose seigneur

was a friend of Raymond de Toulouse, and razed its defences. The Hundred Years War found Beynac in the French camp. In 1360, the Brétigny treaty transferred it by right to English rule but eight years later, it returned to the fore of the fighting on the side of Charles V. The English were never able to capture the citadel. In 1370, the sole heiress of the fief, a three-year-old girl is promised in marriage to her uncle, Pons de Commarque who drove the English out of the Sarlat region and became the most powerful seigneur in Périgord.

Protected naturally by the sheer cliff face on the river side, the castle's defences were reinforced to the north — **a double enceinte, two moats and two barbicans**. We shall start our visit with this face. Built, altered and embellished between the 13th and 18th centuries, it is presented by Jean Secret as "the synthesis of the art of building and the art of self-defence through the centuries". On either side of the strong 13th century **dungeon** stand the main buildings; one dating back to the 13th century and touched up in the 16th and 17th centuries, the other dating back to the 14th and 17th centuries and containing the living quarters. Inside, the **grand States room**, where the Périgord nobility gathered, has ribbed vaults and a sculpted Renaissance fireplace. The walls of the **oratory** are decorated with 14th century frescos.

Beynac, perched on a cliff-top,
watches over the valley and its castles.

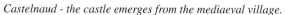
Castelnaud - the castle emerges from the mediaeval village.

Castelnaud Castle houses the Mediaeval War museum.

Painted in a naive style and mixing characters from different periods, a common feature in the Middle Ages, they represent the Last Supper in which Saint Martial plays the role of the head waiter, Christ at the foot of the cross, and the seigneurs of Beynac. The apartments are decorated with 18th century painted ceilings and woodwork. The dungeon is accessed via a narrow staircase and low door. Here we discover an exciting panoramic view of the whole valley and its castles — **Castelnaud, Fayrac** (15th and 17th centuries) and **Marqueyssac** (15th and 17th centuries, gardens). At the cliff's edge, the stone-roofed **castle chapel** dates back to the Romanesque period. Further down, a visit must be made to the **Protohistoric museum** (5000 to 50 years B.C.).

CASTELNAUD
(12 km S.W. of Sarlat)

Guardian of the confluence of the Dordogne and the Céou, that natural passage between Quercy and Périgord, **Castelnaud Castle** appears to rise up out of the mediaeval village pressing to storm the slopes of the hill. This witness to a troubled past is **open to visitors**. Climbing up through the village of old Périgord-style stone-roofed houses, some of which are sculpted, we are suddenly faced with the enormous white stone mass of the castle.

Its foundations goes back to the 12th century. With natural protection being provided on one side by the sheer cliff over the Dordogne, the northern face was reinforced in the 15th century by a barbican to protect the drawbridge.

As the access road to the village constituted a weak point in its defences, a curtain flanked by two towers was added in the 15th century. To the south, the oldest part of the castle, dating back to the 13th century, is arranged in a triangle around a **tall dungeon** guarded by a vast **round artillery tower** with four metre thick walls, built around 1500. The dates speak for themselves. Castelnaud offers visitors a most authentic journey to the heart of a Middle Age fort. At the castle, a visit may be made to the remarkable **Mediaeval War Museum** which houses a collection of weapons and armour and life-sized reconstructions of war machines.

Founded in the 12th century, Castelnaud became the fief of the cruel Cathar, **Bernard de Casnac**, in the 13th century. In 1214, and again the following year, the no less cruel Simon de Montfort took possession of the castle and dismantled it. The rivalry between Castelnaud and Beynac pushed these two neighbours into opposite camps during the **Hundred Years War**. By 1259, Castelnaud had already recognised the suzerainty of the Duke of Aquitaine and King of England, Henry III. In the course of the conflict, the castle which was to remain the most advanced English stronghold to the east of the Guienne, changed hands several times. The English were to conquer it five times. The Caumonts, who had acquired Castelnaud through marriage in 1368, joined the English side in 1405. Several English captains, including the famous **Ramonet de Sort**, held the fortress

for 25 years. It was not until 1442, eleven years before the end of the conflict, that the French took it back following a siege ordered by Charles VII. **Brandelis de Caumont** and his son rebuilt the castle in the second half of the 15th century.

Towards the end of the same century, **François de Caumont** and his wife, Claude de Cardaillac, left the austere fortress and had the Château des Milandes built. At the beginning of the Wars of Religion, as the Caumonts were Protestant, Castelnaud was held by the famous captain **Geoffroy de Vivans**, born at the castle. As the master of Castelnaud, Geoffroy de Caumont, had been assassinated, his daughter, Anne, found herself one of the richest heiresses in the kingdom. Aged eight, she was taken by force from the castle and married against her will to Prince Claude de Carency, a young boy of 13. Five years later, her husband having been killed in a duel, she was hastily remarried to her brother-in-law. Her mother, **Marguerite de Lustrac**, sent the loyal Geoffroy de Vivans to Vauguyon Castle to capture Anne. At the age of 22, wanting to marry (at long last) the man of her heart, she simulated a third kidnapping in order to wed François d'Orléans-Longueville. Castelnaud was fortified once again in the early 17th century by Nompar de Caumont. Abandoned during the Revolution, it was to be used as a stone quarry during the 19th century before a splendid restoration programme was undertaken in 1967. The **Walnut** museum should also be visited in Castelnaud.

The Château des Milandes, where the memory of Josephine Baker is omnipresent.

The North of Black Périgord:
The Vézère Valley

SAINT-AMAND-DE-COLY
(6 km east of Montignac)

As soon as you approach the little village of Saint-Amand, your eyes will inevitably meet the gigantic stone silhouette of the **finest fortified church in Périgord**. Legend has it that an abbey was founded in the seventh century by **Saint Amand**, an anchorite who spread the Gospel throughout Périgord. If this **Romanesque abbey** were of tremendous importance, as illustrated by the size of the buildings, it also experienced a rapid decline. This impressive fortress was occupied by the Huguenots in 1575 and besieged by the seneschal of Périgord and 2000 soldiers who had been battering it for six days.

The church is still surrounded by **walls**, surmounted by a parapet walk. Once inside, you will encounter a huge entrance **porch**

which, from a distance, looks like a mouth ready to devour the village. Lightened by a stained glass window, it culminates in a pointed arch and supports a **defence chamber** which protected the approaches to the portal. The triple arched portal whose capitals are sculpted with foliage, is surmounted by twin telamones from the Romanesque period.

Les Milandes: Josephine Baker established her "world village" in a half-Gothic, half-Renaissance setting.

LES MILANDES
(15 km S.W. of Sarlat)

Situated within the village of Castelnaud, in the middle of tiered grounds overlooking the left bank of the Dordogne, the **Château des Milandes**, whose name remains eternally linked to that of **Josephine Baker**, is **open to visitors**. It was built around 1489 by François de Caumont, Seigneur of Castelnaud, and his wife, Claude de Cardaillac, who preferred to leave behind their austere fortress for a chic residence. Following the Second World War, Les Milandes became the property of Josephine Baker who founded her "**world village**" for abandoned children here. Thanks to her, the dormant village and the surrounding area came back to life.

The château offers a pleasant transition between Gothic and Renaissance styles. The building is flanked by round and square towers with turrets. The gable windows and transom bays are beautifully crowned with ridge ornaments and pediments decorated with blazons. During your visit, you will discover the 70,000 m2 of ornamental **gardens** and **grounds** and a **falconry** museum.

Romanesque sculptures on the abbey in Saint-Amand-de-Coly.

The walls of the southern apsidiole are decorated with applied ornaments and the cornice modillions are sculpted with heads and geometric figures. The apse which is lit up by three bays and an oculus, ends in a defensive terrace. Particular emphasis should be paid to the formidable defences of this abbey, the best preserved in the Périgord region. Apart from the enceinte and the dungeon belfry, **a parapet walk** runs beneath the stone roof and corbels support overhanging **bartizans**. There are also defence chambers above the transept and apse and three defensive buildings at ground level, near the chancel. This highly elaborate system meant that enemies could not only be kept at a distance but also be destroyed if they succeeded in entering the church. The simple, spare interior has the **austere beauty** of Augustinian abbey buildings. The crossing is crowned with a pendentive-supported **cupola** featuring firing holes. The southern apsidiole contains **sculptures** of a rare quality, reminiscent of Souillac — two men devoured by a lion, and a dragon bird. The two bays of the chancel have very old ribbed vaults. **La Cassagne** Templar grange (13th century) and **Chavagnac** dungeon (13th century) should also be visited.

Saint-Amand-de-Coly - the fortified porch surmounted by a defence chamber.

Saint-Amand-de-Coly - a fine, austere stone cross in the heart of Périgord.

Montignac: the remains of the castle on the banks of the Vézère. The village is also the site of the famous

Overleaf - Lascaux (from left to right and from top to bottom)

1 - Red aurochs - main room, right-hand wall.
2 - Great black bull - central recess.
3 - Leaping cow (1.7 m in length). Frieze of little horses - recess, right-hand wall.
4 - Dapple horse.

5 - Ibex and horses in the recess, right-hand wall.
6 - Frieze of deer - left-hand wall of the main room.
7 - Deer (70 cm in length). Close-up of the frieze.
8 - Galloping horse - recess, left-hand wall.
9 - The "Chinese" horse in the recess.

MONTIGNAC and LASCAUX

(25 km north of Sarlat)

A small town of 3,000 inhabitants on the banks of the river Vézère, Montignac owes its fame to the discovery in 1940 of the **"eighth wonder of the world", the Lascaux cave**. It is difficult to imagine what the **castle** used to be like in Montignac, the **military capital** of Périgord, when you see what remains — a dungeon and a few pieces of wall which the town seems to have devoured.

Montignac still has a number of old houses around Place d'Armes, in addition to the Périgord folk museum and the **Eugène-Le Roy museum** where the writer's room has been recreated. **Eugène Le Roy** (1836-1907), Périgord's greatest writer, is most certainly the one who has best translated, in basic yet engaging language, the landscape of his region and the harsh living conditions of his contemporaries. Born in Hautefort, he was a student in Périgueux and already a fierce Republican. He became a collector of taxes, a post which enabled him to discover his region of birth and to stay in Montignac for the very first time. Appointed to Hautefort, he published his first novel *Le Moulin du Frau*, in 1893. Others followed including two which were set in the Montignac region, *Mademoiselle de la Ralphie*, and his masterpiece, *Jacquou le Croquant*, published in 1900, which Stellio Lorenzi brought to the whole nation in 1969 through the medium

of television. In 1902, **Le Roy** retired to Montignac where he wrote *Au Pays des Pierres*, *L'Année Rustique en Périgord* and his final novel, published after his death, in 1911, and considered to be one of the best, *L'Ennemi de la Mort*. He was buried without religious ceremony, the French flag draped over his coffin.

Around Montignac, you will discover the rustic charm of the Château de la **Grande-Filolie** (15th and 17th centuries), the Château de **Rastignac**, the image of the White House in Washington, and the pretty village of **Saint-Geniès** where the tiny Chapelle du Cheylard is decorated with 14th century frescos. Further up the Vézère, visits may be made to **Terrasson** (13th century bridge) and **Condat** (15th century hospital commandery). Towards Périgueux, you will be able to see the Château d'**Ajat**, formerly possessed by the Knights Templars which is open to visitors, and Carcassou Abbey in **Bauzens**. The Gothic church in **La Douze** features a sculpted altar.

LASCAUX

Two kilometres to the south, we reach the most important stage of our journey through Prehistory — **Lascaux cave**. Its fortuitous discovery was something of a fairy tale. On 12th September 1940, four young boys decided to explore a cavity on

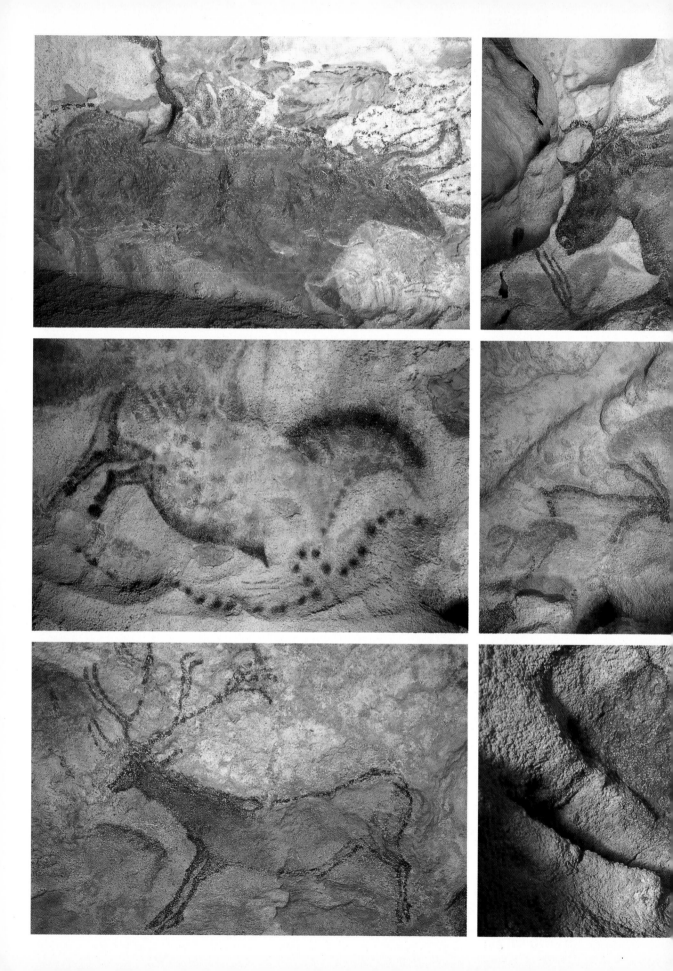

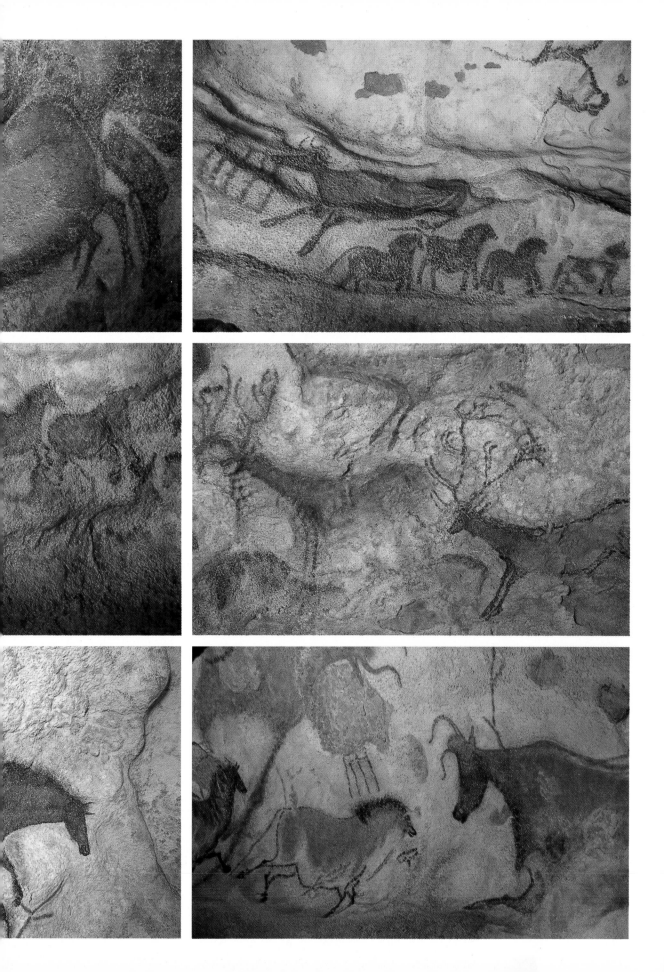

Lascaux hill. Legend had it that an underground passage with hidden treasure linked this spot to Montignac castle. They did indeed find **treasure** — Lascaux cave, the finest of all prehistoric painted caves. The age of Lascaux was long debated by experts. Prehistorians now agree on dating the paintings between the end of the Solutrean period and the beginning of the Magdalenian period, in other words around **15000 years B.C.** Artists from the Palaeolithic Age found in the cave's subsoil the three fundamental colours in the **prehistoric palette** — manganese dioxide for black and iron oxides for the yellow and red ochres. Excavations have revealed their lighting system — around a hundred grease lamps made of stone. Three painting techniques were used, line drawing with a finger or crayon, dabbing with tufts of hair or clumps of moss and dye spraying through a hollow bone or a blowpipe.

Let's now enter the sanctuary. The first step into the **main bull room** is thrilling. A ring of animals springs to life, with four large bulls dominating a flight of horses or deer. All of these animals seem in fact to move as you advance into the room. The prehistoric artists have concentrated them along an imaginary line, half way up the wall, making use of the **relief** of the rock. A calcite hole gives life to the gaze of a deer, a hump depicts a back or a stomach, or brings out the breast muscles. The first painting in the room already queries the observer — the skin of a panther, the tail of a deer, the hump of a bison, two horns, it is the famous **unicorn**, which is pregnant yet given male genitals. Is it an imaginary animal, or rather, as certain historians have cautiously put forward, the "**sorcerer**" of Lascaux, as would appear to be confirmed by the human legs and a face from which only the muzzle needs to be removed ? Let's not forget that in prehistory, all explanations are only ever a hypothesis. Stopping at the four bulls, we see that they are, in fact, **aurochs**, a race which disappeared in France in the Middle Ages. These huge paintings, one of which measures 5.5 metres, gives an impression of life and

power to the room. This "presence" is created thanks to the **twisted perspective**, an artistic effect which presents the animals in profile with a three-quarter view of their horns. This technique, used throughout the Upper Palaeolithic Age, does not indicate that the artists were incompetent but quite the contrary; it shows their great skill in representing life.

Opposite the entrance, a narrow alley — the central recess — opens up. This is where we find the finest paintings in the cave and the painted ceiling which led Father Breuil to name it "**The Prehistoric Sistine Chapel**". Here the painters have not systematically sought to achieve a realistic image, but have created true compositions such as the "cluster of red cows" whose heads form a circle. The two main coloured figures face each other, a strong black **bull** which is reminiscent of Cretan art and a cow which seems to leap before a grid traced at its hoofs. Horses are represented in a variety of forms. The famous conventionalised "**Chinese**" **horse** enables us to appreciate more thoroughly the technique of these artists. The stomach, partially coated in ochre, fills out. In the medium ground, the legs detached from the body create an effect of perspective. This technique was not to be rediscovered until the Renaissance period.

Returning to the main room and taking a second passage off to the left, we reach **the "nave"**, a vast cavity where the paintings have suffered from the ravages of time more than anywhere else. A large black cow dominates the scene by its size and two bisons, with stunningly wild density and blind fury, flee as if startled by the visitor. On the opposite side, a frieze of five deer which appear to be swimming presents a most gentle image. A corridor with difficult access leads to a small closet featuring several carvings, particularly of felines. Finally, a reinforcement of the nave — the apse — the walls of which are covered with a mass of carvings, opens out into a **pit**. Four metres below, this pit has another enigma in store for us. What is the meaning of this injured bison spilling its guts, this rhinoceros, this bird

The Régourdou bear.

Régourdou - the site.

perched on a stick and this naked man, with an erect penis, drawn in a child-like manner?

Miraculously preserved by a totally impermeable marl roof, Lascaux was doubly struck by **disease** unwittingly brought in by visitors — firstly green scale, a proliferation of algae, then white disease, the accelerated formation of calcite. In 1963, the cave was closed to the public. Treated like an invalid, it has now regained its sparkle but can no longer open its doors due to the danger of a relapse.

Le Thot - reconstruction of a prehistoric hut of mammoth bones discovered in Siberia.

Ten years of work were required to produce a facsimile, **Lascaux II**, on the initiative of the Dordogne District Council. Using computers, the caves were reconstructed to within a millimetre by Renaud Sanson. The paintings, produced using natural dyes and according to prehistoric techniques, were the work of Monique Peytral. The facsimile is a **masterpiece** in itself. Indeed, only specialists would be able to affirm that they were not in the real cave. The entrance has been converted into a **museum**.

Located a few hundred yards from Lascaux, but **55,000 years** further back in time, the **Régourdou** site (open to visitors) has led to the discovery of a skeleton of a Neanderthal man and a very large quantity of bear bones. Today, it is inhabited by bears which are very much alive.

Five kilometres to the west, on the edge of Barade forest, the pretty Périgord **village** of **Fanlac** found fame when **Stellio Lorenzi** located the house of the parish priest, Father Bonal, here for his production of *Jacquou le Croquant*. "Combenègre", the residence of Eugène Le Roy's young hero, is situated not far

from the village. Following the broadcast of the TV series, veritable pilgrimages were organised to the village. It is true that Fanlac is not lacking in charm with its well and its fortified **Romanesque church**. A 17th century cusped, sculpted cross stands in the square. The 14th and 15th century manor house was the residence of the knight of Galibert in *Jacquou*.

THONAC: LE THOT and LOSSE
(6 km S.W. of Montignac)

One kilometre to the north of Thonac, the ***Centre d'art préhistorique du Thot*** is **open to visitors**. Built in 1972, on the initiative of the Dordogne tourist board, this provides an excellent initiation to Prehistory. It includes a zoological park presenting "survivors" of prehistoric wildlife (bison, tarpans, deer, etc.), film and slide shows on the techniques of artists of the Palaeolithic Age, mouldings of objects, reconstructions of the finest cave paintings and life-sized, articulated models of a mammoth and a woolly rhinoceros. One kilometre to the north, the **Château de Losse** is **open to visitors**. It occupies an **exceptional site**, on a small cliff into which a vast cave had been cut, where the architect had the audacity to build a stone arch to support the veranda. At the foot of the rocks, the dark waters of the Vézère reflect the silhouette of the residence. We enter the property through a well protected 17th century **gatehouse**, roofed in

Le Thot - articulated mammoth.

A bison at Le Thot.

The Château de Losse gatehouse.

The Romanesque church in Saint-Léon-sur-Vézère.

stone and preceded by a drawbridge. A curtain crowned with watch towers and turrets stands beside the drawbridge. The residence is still surrounded by moats and ramparts. Having admired the fine **façade** with its Renaissance windows, we enter the building via a flight of magnificent stone steps.

SAINT-LÉON-SUR-VÉZÈRE
(9 km S.W. of Montignac)

The Montignac to Les Eyzies road runs by the beautiful little **village** of Saint-Léon, which is certainly worth a detour. The site was occupied in ancient times as the church rests on **Gallo-Roman** sub-foundations which are perfectly visible from the riverside. Roofed in stone, the cruciform 11th century **Romanesque church**, dedicated to Saint Leontius, ends in a half dome apse flanked by two apsidioles. The apse is decorated with five applied arches extending into columns with sculpted capitals. The vaults of the apse and the southern apsidiole feature frescos from several periods. In its rural setting on the banks of the river, standing on a small, peaceful square, the church is one of the oldest in the Périgord. It was remarkably restored in 1965. The **balance** of the whole church and the perfect **harmony** of its apse mark it out as one of the finest. You should also take the opportunity of wandering through the narrow streets and slipping in be-

Saint-Léon-sur-Vézère: Château de Clérans and church belfry.

Below: The hosanna cross in Sergeac.

tween the old houses of the village, brought to life in the summer by the chords of the classical **music festival**. By the roadside, the **Château de La Salle**, standing in the centre of a park, features a square 14th century dungeon with a stone roof. Beyond, the high roofs of the 16th century **Château de Clérans** appear with their weather-vanes and pedimented gable windows. At the edge of the village, the cemetery conceals 13th century recess tombs and a beautiful Gothic-style **expiatory chapel** which has been recently restored. The spandrel of the chapel door is decorated with a most strange inscription in the Occitan language recalling an extraordinary event witnessed by the village. In the time of Saint Louis, in 1233, a servant passing in front of the cemetery fired a bolt from a crossbow at the crucifix which guarded the entrance. Blood spurted out and the man fell stone dead with his face turned "back-to-front". This is how the legend goes, but it is really a **legend**? In 1890, the tomb of the profaner was opened by the serious-minded Périgord historic and archaeological society. They discovered a skeleton with the skull turned round.

SERGEAC and CASTELMERLE
(9 km S.W. of Montignac)

Facing the rocky spur of the **Château de Belcayre**, the little **village** of Sergeac has retained a remarkable degree of unity.

Before reaching the entrance to the village, at the crossroads, a fine 15th century sculpted **hosanna cross** depicting Christ, the Virgin Mary, Saint Michael and a Knight whose shield is embossed with salamanders announces that you are approaching a centre of Périgord culture. Built on former Gallo-Roman property, a church which belonged to Sarlat Abbey stood here as early as 1053. In 1275, this is where the **Knights Templars** established an important **commandery** which quickly prospered. Five years later, Hélie Rudel, the powerful seigneur of Bergerac and Montignac, sold them some land and his legal rights over Sergeac.

The members of this religious and military order installed the residence of their **Grand Master** for Périgord here. With their stone roofs, the white houses in the village are grouped around a 14th and 15th century **manor**,

The Château de Belcayre.

the former house of the commander, a simple building standing alongside a round machicolated tower and preceded by a fortified gate. One kilometre from the village, a vast ***enceinte*** provides a reminder of the place where the commandery was erected. In the heart of Sergeac, the scant style of the fine 12th century **Romanesque church** shows a Templar influence.

L'église templière de Sergeac.

Like the majority of villages in the Vézère valley, Sergeac is an important **prehistoric** centre. Let's go down, slightly to the west of the village, to **Castelmerle** vale where the shelters are **open to visitors**. After Les Eyzies, this was the most densely populated area of Black Périgord during the Palaeolithic Age. Its **nine shelters** were occupied from 30,000 to 10,000 years B.C. and have revealed a number of works of art and tools. The **Blanchard I shelter**, occupied in the Aurignacian period (30,000-25,000 years B.C.), discovered in 1910 and then studied by Breuil, has provided twenty blocks with animal carvings occasionally overlaid with paint, as well as blocks with rings and cups. **Le Roc d'Acier** features Périgord-style and Solutrean dwellings. The **Labattut shelter** has preserved traces of a fireplace and a flint cutting workshop. Here one can see reproductions of paintings and carvings which decorated the ceiling some 20,000 years ago. The **Reverdit shelter** includes a low-relief sculpture of five animals from the Magdalenian period. The habitat of Cro-Magnon hunters, the **Souquette shelter** has revealed a number of bones and tools. A visit may be made to the so-called **"Englishman's" cave fort** (*Fort troglodytique des Anglais*) at the same time as the Reverdit shelter.

On a huge natural terrace, the cave fort at La Roque-Saint-Christophe.

PEYZAC-LE MOUSTIER
and LA ROQUE-SAINT-CHRISTOPHE
(10 km N.E. of Les Eyzies)

It is **Prehistory**, omnipresent as in Les Eyzies, which has made the renown of this community. The famous **Le Moustier shelter, open to visitors,** gave its name to the Mousterian period. It consists of two shelters, excavated successively by Lartet in 1864 and by Peyrony, each presenting examples of Mousterian with Acheulian traditions, typical Mousterian covering the period from 100,000 to 35,000 years B.C., Chatelperronian, a period of transition during which modern man appeared, and ancient Aurignacian (-30,000 years). The second shelter revealed the skeleton of an adolescent Neanderthal man.

One kilometre to the west, at the **"Pas du Miroir"**, where the road runs between the cliff and the river and threads its way through the rocks, one may visit one of the most exceptional sites in Périgord, **La Roque-Saint-Christophe**, which looks down on to the river Vézère. Five storeys, 80 m in height, 500 m in length, and a remarkable **cave fort** make this site a must for all lovers of prehistory and archaeology. This **vast natural terrace**, one of the largest in Europe, was inhabited as early as the Mousterian period (-70,000 years). It provided shelter in turn for Cro-Magnon man, and people of the Neolithic period, the Bronze Age (1500 B.C.), the Iron Age (800 B.C.), the Gallo-Roman period and the Middle Ages. The site which visitors may discover today is a giant

Le Moustier shelter,
a site which lent its name to the Mousterian period.

troglodytic chain to which only the ones in Cappadoce, Turkey, can be compared.

The cave fort was built by **Frotaire**, bishop of Périgueux in the tenth century, to prevent the Vikings from sailing up the Vézère. Once through the original entrance to the fort, we discover the rocks specked with thousands of square niches into which the beams which supported the houses were inserted. The **shelters** feature receptacles dug into the rock, ducts to collect and drain away water and **rings** cut into the stone (1500 altogether) which were used for hanging up animals and lamps. Some of the "rooms" had a specific purpose (abattoir, smoke room, safe, etc.). The village itself, suspended over five terraces, could provide shelter for 1000 to 1500 inhabitants. Just imagine it swarming with activity, the merchants'stores and the craftsmen's workshops. The **church** can still be made out from its engraved crosses and tombs. From the terrace, a vast panorama opens out over the Vézère.

Above Le Mostier, on the **Côte de Jor** (panorama), we shall be able to discover **Chabans** castle, the centre of **Tibetan buddhism** of Dagpo Kagyuling, and the 13th century leaning tower of **La Vermondie**.

La Vézère, "valley of Man".
Panoramic view of the Côte de Jor, near Le Moustier.

Rouffignac. Mammoth and ibexes on the main ceiling in the "Grotte des Cent Mammouths".

ROUFFIGNAC -
The Hundred Mammoths and Herm Castle
(16 km north of Les Eyzies)

Five kilometres to the south of Rouffignac, tourists have the chance to take a marvellous **journey to the centre of the earth**, by visiting the *Grotte des Cent Mammouths* (the Cave of a Hundred Mammoths). No carbide lamps as in Jules Verne's time, but a little **electric train**.

This vast cave with over eight kilometres of passages has never been closed and has been receiving visitors since the 16th century. Although explored by illustrious prehistorians such as Martel, Breuil and Glory, its paintings were only revealed in 1956 by Nougier and Robert. If many claimed that they were a hoax at the time, their authenticity is no longer questioned today. The paintings date back to the **middle and late Magdalenian** periods, 11000 years B.C. Digs at the entrance have revealed a human presence at the end of prehistoric times (Tardenoisian, Sauveterrian, Neolithic and Iron Age).

A long time before the appearance of artwork, man had to contend with **bears** for the possession of these caverns. The lairs and claw marks still provide evidence of their passage. The first drawings are to be found 800 metres from the entrance and they continue to the very bottom of the galleries.

The cave owes its name to some **150** figures of **mammoths**, of which it contains half of the known representations alone. It is curious to note that this mammoth sanctuary dates back to a period when the beast was becoming extinct in the region, like the woolly rhinoceros illustrated in a frieze.

The mammoth is sometimes represented quite realistically, such as the famous "**patriarch**" whose back is marked with ritual symbols, but sometimes only the outline is traced. Near a pit, the artist has illustrated an encounter between two herds. The little train stops at the entrance to the main room where the painted **ceiling**, decorated with a composition of horses, bison, ibexes and mammoths, is the masterpiece of Rouffignac.

Five kilometres to the north, **Herm Castle is open to visitors** who are not afraid to encounter ghosts straight out of an authentic **Shakespearean drama**. A little dirt track leads to the castle which is now but a rather impressive **ruin** struck, it would seem, by divine punishment.

Rouffignac – the woolly rhinoceros. Like its contemporary, the mammoth, it roamed across our region before disappearing around 10,000 years B.C.

In 1513, **Jean III de Calvimont**, future ambassador to Francis I, had the original fortress converted. The "three knocks" opening the tragedy began with the violent, mysterious death of the son of the builder of Herm who left his three-year-old daughter, **Marguerite**, as his only heiress. His widow, **Anne d'Abzac**, guided more through interest than sentiment, not only wanted to be remarried to Foucault d'Aubusson but also appropriate the inheritance. She therefore compelled her daughter to marry François, the son of Foucault. The years passed by without bringing joy to this forced marriage. François fell in love with a certain **Marie d'Hautefort**, aunt of the "Aurora" of Louis XIII, and had but one idea — to get rid of Marguerite. He apparently had no difficulty in obtaining the complicity of his mother-in-law to carry out this macabre plan. One day in February 1605, he discharged all the servants, forced Marguerite to sign a letter which stripped her of all her assets and had her strangled.

François did not, however, get away with it as easily as that. An autopsy was called for and a number of witnesses came forward. Gripped with fear, if not remorse, Anne d'Abzac accused her son-in-law of murdering her daughter. François no longer went out without an armed guard who made short work of the soldiers sent to arrest him. The affair dragged on and François, still free, married Marie d'Hautefort in 1606.

Three years after the murder, Anne d'Abzac, who had not lost interest, agreed to withdraw her complaint against a part of her daughter's inheritance, but her entourage, particularly the **Calvimonts** of Saint-Martial, cried shame and forced her to pursue the murderer. **François d'Aubusson** gave himself up in Paris and died at the Conciergerie a few years later.

Unfortunately, the affair did not stop there. Marie d'Hautefort showed that she had a character which was just as hardened as that of Anne d'Abzac. Through the assassination of the two Saint-Martial brothers, she legally obtained ownership of the castle. But as blood begets blood, her son Charles was murdered. In the search for protection, Marie married **Raphaël de Baudet**, a former accomplice and, renewing a previous scenario, promised the hand of her daughter, Françoise, to his son. Françoise was however already engaged to Godefroy de la Roche-Aymon. The two suitors fought a duel and, against all expectations, Godefroy killed his opponent. By entering the family, he also entered his mother-in-law's service because he killed a Calvimont who had had the audacity to marry the widow of Marie's murdered son. In 1641, Françoise died in childbirth. As Marie's stooge, Raphaël de Baudet organised the

murder of Charles de Caumont, a brother-in-law with whom she had fallen out, but he died during the shooting which he had set up. The years passed by without a glimmer of light. Françoise's daughter lost her first husband at war, and her second was to be murdered. As for Marie d'Hautefort, she died a natural death at the accursed castle. Herm was finally to be bought in 1682 by another Marie d'Hautefort, of fonder memory, and let to a farm-er.

TURSAC, LA MADELEINE and PREHISTOPARC
(5 km N.E. of Les Eyzies)

The little village of Tursac is one of the main prehistoric centres in Périgord. Facing the village, on the right bank of the Vézère at water level, the great shelter of La Madeleine, which gave its name to the Magdalenian period, offers hikers the charm of its rural setting. Digs beginning in 1863 by Lartet, and continued by Peyrony, have revealed many implements, fine examples

Left: The ruins of Herm castle.

Right: Lookout post at La Madeleine (Tursac).

of furniture and a child's skeleton. Above all, they have allowed scientists to establish the full chronology of the middle and upper Magdalenian periods, occupation of the site spreading as far as the Azilian era, in other words from 12,000 to 8000 years B.C.

The prehistoric part of La Madeleine is closed to the public, but no-one will regret a **visit** to the **cave fort** and the remains of the **castle**. Here, as at several points throughout Périgord, the prehistoric level was succeeded by a village of the early Middle Ages (tenth century), dug into the rock and fortified to withstand Viking raids. In this vast troglodyte village, which was still occupied in the 17th century, one cannot fail to notice the 15th century **chapel** where legend conceals treasure, and an "overhead *cluzeau*" or "lookout post". These lookout posts were used to communicate from fort to fort by means of light signals and to call for help in the event of attack. The visit will reveal the village's defence system and the day-to-day life of our cave-dwelling

The cave fort of La Madeleine (Tursac).

Scenes from prehistoric life at Prehistoparc: mammoth hunting and day-to-day life.

ancestors. The hill is crowned by the mediaeval castle of **Petit Marzac**, a third level which completes this fine example of the sustainability of life through centuries and millennia.

Near Tursac, visits may be made to the **Cellier** and **Pagès** shelters, the hamlet of **Le Ruth** and, above all, **Préhistoparc**. Here, **reconstructed scenes of prehistoric life** are presented in a natural setting — mammoth hunting, cutting up of flint, burial, woolly rhinoceros on the charge, etc.

LES EYZIES
(21 km west of Sarlat)

It is commonplace for Les Eyzies to be introduced as the **world's prehistoric capital** and the numerous painted caves and, particularly, the proliferation of rock shelters only confirm this notion. The most varied prehistoric, and historic, styles and periods are represented, making Les Eyzies the archetypal **town for travelling through the past**. This

Les Eyzies: cliff and museum.

Above: National Prehistory Museum,
Les Eyzies, and primitive man by the sculptor Dardé.

The Roc de Tayac.

vast, motionless promenade will enable us to appreciate more thoroughly the passing of prehistoric time. From La Micoque to Laugerie-Basse, from 300,000 to 5000 years B.C., prehistory at Les Eyzies lasted sixty times longer than history and one hundred and fifty times longer than the Christian era.

Even if you only have a passing interest in prehistoric times, Les Eyzies would be worth a visit, if only for its **site**. At the confluence of the Vézère and the Beune, the little village, out of which rises an old castle converted into a museum, clings to the bottom of tall cliffs containing shelters, caves and **troglodyte** dwellings, crowned with green oaks and juniper trees. Having crossed the Vézère, a little road which winds between the river and the rocks follows the prehistoric **"Royal road"**; an unimaginable succession of caves and shelters in an impressive framework of cliffs.

The National Prehistory Museum

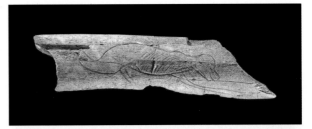

Bought by the French government in 1913, at the instance of Peyrony, Les Eyzies Castle, itself built on a prehistoric site and a troglodyte village, became the prehistory museum in 1918. Today, its collections include around **a million objects**. The clear way in which they are represented and the full range of treasures which it contains make this museum quite easy to follow and fascinating for visitors. The visit begins on the third floor with the "Land of cut stones", presented in chronological order. The second floor of the dungeon is essentially devoted to art. The first floor contains maps, chronological charts and explanations. On the ground floor, the Renaissance building includes a recap of early discoveries, excavation methods and a description of certain sites. A vast programme of work aims to increase its visitor capacity considerably.

Before leaving, let's go out on to the terrace to take in the splendid panoramic view and say hello to the museum's stone guardian, the famous **"primitive man"**, avoiding the traditional error of mistaking him for "Cro-Magnon" man. He might get cross.

Painted caves

FONT-DE-GAUME: On leaving Les Eyzies along the Sarlat road, a steep path up a cliff side, followed by a narrow, distorted entrance which looks as if it were meant to illustrate a Jules Verne novel, or a Walt Disney film, take us to Font-de-Gaume. The cave, **open to the public**, proposes a fine selection

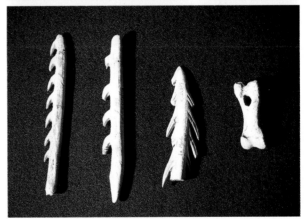

Facing page, from top to bottom:
The ithyphallic sorcerer of La Madeleine (Magdalenian IV), around 14,000 years old.
Solutrean "laurel leaves", cut flint around 20,000 years old.
Magdalenian harpoons and, on the right, a whistle.
Following pages: Les Eyzies, the world's prehistoric capital - general view.

Font-de-Gaume: two specimens from the frieze of bison.

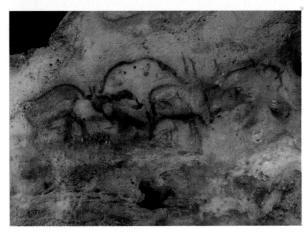

Font-de-Gaume (Les Eyzies): painted horse and bison, partially covered with calcite.
Top - Les Combarelles (Les Eyzies): "The drinking reindeer". The dark cavity could represent
the depths of the water.

of **carvings** and polychrome **paintings**, the majority of which date back to the **Magdalenian** period (-12,000 years). Some 60 metres under ground, the passage reaches a narrowing, the "Rubicon", which marks the start of the painted section. This is indicated by the red spots on the left-hand wall.

Similarly, a series of small rods marks the bottom of the gallery. Once the Rubicon has been "crossed", we discover the first frieze of a dozen mammoths and bison. Here, engraving and painting are brought together. Further on, near the junction, on the left, we discover the famous scene of the **reindeer face to**

face, a large male leaning over a female, legs folded. On the right, in the side recess, we discover several bison, reindeer and horses, partially damaged by the calcite. Returning to the main gallery, a large frieze of five carved and painted bison, stand out against a white calcite background. At the back of the gallery, in a hollow named "**the bison's chapel**", a dozen or so representations include four polychrome bison.

LES COMBARELLES: Discovered in 1901 and subsequently studied by Capitan, Breuil and Peyrony, Les

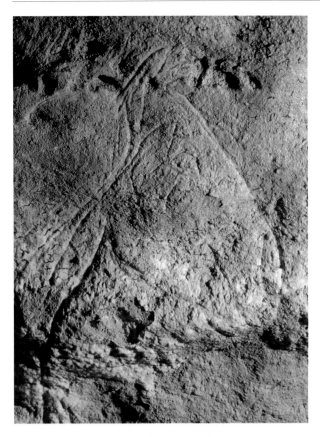

Combarelles cave — which is also **open to the public** — is situated by the Sarlat road, 1500 metres from Font-de-Gaume. Some **800 engravings** are spread along the 300 metres of this winding underground alley. The walls over the final 120 metres are covered with a riot of tangled carvings — mammoths, ibexes, kiangs, bears, reindeer, does, woolly rhinoceros, bison and horses. The horse is largely predominant — over 140 may be made out. These engravings date back to the middle and late phases of **Magdalenian** period (from 12,000 to 10,000 years B.C.). The cave is also well known for its numerous human representations, 48 in all. Amongst the cave's other curiosities, one can admire the carving of a **lioness**, a kiang, an ibex, one of Les Combarelles'rare paintings, and particularly the one of a **reindeer** stretching out to drink.

Two kilometres to the south of Les Eyzies, **La Mouthe** cave, discovered in 1891, contains **carvings** touched up with lines of ochre. These works spread from the **Gravettian** period (25,000 years) to the late **Magdalenian** period (-10,000 years). The main curiosity involves what one believes to be the carved and painted representation of a prehistoric hut.

Facing page: Les Combarelles (Les Eyzies) - Carved horse head. Below: Les Eyzies museum. 1 - Items of jewellery: bears' and carnivores' teeth; left, eyed needles; top, coloured crayons from the Palaeolithic era. 2 - Necklace of perforated teeth from the Fourneau du Diable, upper Solutrean era (reconstruction), National Prehistory Museum. 3 - Heads of spears, arrows, etc., of various periods and origins. 4 - Les Eyzies: Pataud shelter.

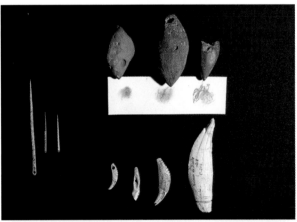

2

4

The shelters

We shall now present the main shelters where the populations of Les Eyzies lived, by chronological order of dwelling, showing an apparent line of continuity.

The **La Micoque** site has not only given its name to Micoquian, the contemporary industrial period of the early Mousterian era (100,000 years B.C.), but its lowest level has also yielded a few flints, cut by the first inhabitants of Les Eyzies, which are much older as they date back more than 300,000 years.

But it was in the **Aurignacian** period (30,000 years B.C.), with the arrival of *Homo Sapiens Sapiens*, that Les Eyzies and its surroundings really experienced a demographic boom and became the centre of the prehistoric world. This Aurignacian man who chose the Périgord to live and create the first works of art, is known to us by the name of **Cro-Magnon man**. The Cro-Magnon **shelter**, near the hotel of the same name, was the place where five skeletons were discovered surrounded by jewels and shells, in 1868. An examination of the skeletons by Lartet revealed a human type of large size (around 1.80 m) and quite similar to us, both in terms of physique and his cranial capacity.

The vale of *Gorge d'Enfer* (Hell Gorge), **open to visitors**, contains several small caves and a huge rock shelter. Still in the *Val d'Enfer* (Hell Valley), the shelter known as *Le Poisson* (The

Moulding of the skull of "Madame" Pataud, around 23,000 years old, at the Pataud shelter site museum.

Fish) consists of an initial Aurignacian level, but the **sculpture** of the **large salmon** made in the ceiling dates back to the Gravettian (-25,000 years) or upper Perigordian (-30,000 years).

The fourteen archaeological levels of the **Pataud shelter** cover the Aurignacian, Gravettian and ancient Solutrean periods (-32,000 to -18,000 years). A remarkable **site museum** provides information boards, showcases, videos and animated models for visitors. Discover with emotion the skeleton of a 16 year old

Gorge d'Enfer (Les Eyzies): the Abri du Poisson. This 1.1 m long salmon, 25,000 years old, is one of the rare representations of a fish in cave paintings.

Bone carvings of mammoth trunks and feet, found in Laugerie-Haute, date back some 16,000 years to the ancient Magdalenian period. Preserved at the National Prehistory Museum.

woman, dead for over 20,000 years, as well as her recreated bronze statue. The ceiling of the shelter features a sculpted ibex.

Laugerie-Haute, open to visitors, acted as a standard metre to establish prehistoric chronology thanks to its **42 sedimentological levels**, the remains of which are presented to the public. Occupied as early as the end of the Perigordian period (20,000 years B.C.), it is particularly characteristic of the Solutrean era (20,000 to 15,000 years B.C.) of which it possesses all the stratigraphic series. It was abandoned in the Magdalenian period fol-

lowing the collapse of its upper terrace around 14,000 years B.C.

The first shelter at the **Laugerie-Basse** site, **open to visitors**, has yielded numerous implements dating back to the middle and upper Magdalenian and Azilian periods, from 12,000 to 8000 years B.C. After Lartet's excavations in 1864, a skeleton surrounded by shells was found in 1872. The second, the Marseilles shelter, covers a wider period. The whole of the Magdalenian era, from 15,000 to 10,000 years B.C., is present here.

Let's go back through history to visit **Tayac church**, built as a **fortress** by the monks of Paunat abbey in the 12th century.

On the other side of the Vézère, the **Roc de Tayac** was initially a **cave fort** before becoming a fortress and toll station for the ferrymen in the lower Middle Ages. Converted into a panoramic restaurant at the beginning of the century, it now houses the **Museum of speleology**. Exhibits include explorers'equipment and specimens of cavern fauna accompanied by explanatory charts. Hidden amongst the prehistoric sites above Laugerie-Basse, the **Grand Roc cave** may also be **visited**. Discovered in 1924, it conceals a number of fine "eccentric" concretions which bear a striking resemblance to coral.

On the Périgueux road, beyond Laugerie-Haute, **Manaurie** has another **cave, Carpe-Diem, open to visitors,** which features coloured stalactites.

Concretions in Grand-Roc cave, Les Eyzies.

SIREUIL and COMMARQUE
(7 km east of Les Eyzies)

Above the valleys of the two branches of the river **Beune**, tributaries of the Vézère, the little village of Sireuil has a number of significant **prehistoric** sites. **Sireuil** is particularly known for being the home of the **C.P.I.E.** (Centre Permanant d'Initiation à l'Environnement), which organises a number of training courses, essentially in the areas of history and ecology.

The most famous stone huts (known as bories) in the whole of Périgord, **"the Gallic huts of Le Breuil"**, are to be found around 7 km south-east of Sireuil, near the hamlet of Bénivès. Built near to a farm where they are used as sheep pens, they form a curious little group of buildings. Incorrectly referred to as "Gallic", they were erected at an undetermined time. This type of rural construction was practised from 3000 years B.C. until the 19th century. The **film industry** could not ignore such a wonderful site. The cameras of Stellio Lorenzi, for *Jacquou le Croquant*, and Robert Hossein, for *Les Misérables*, came to film these picturesque bories.

Sireuil church.

Stone hut at the Camp au Combal, Sireuil.

Four kilometres to the east of Sireuil, difficult of access, isolated from the surrounding hamlets by a thick forest and overlooking a marshy valley crossed by the Beune, **Commarque** seems to be something of a shadow of a castle. A perfect example of a Périgord mediaeval **fortress**, it is now an enormous **ruin** invaded, even a short time ago, by the trees and hawthorns. Its high dungeon dominates the rest of a village once surrounded by huge ramparts.

The site has been occupied for many centuries since a **prehistoric cave** is to be found beneath the castle. This conceals a sculpted horse, reminiscent of its "neighbours" of Cap-Blanc. The **cliff** between the cave and the enormous 13th century castle is riddled with a network of shelters and the remains of **cave fort**, excavated probably around the ninth or tenth century. This succession of dwellings, like a long slice of human history frozen in time, some 500 years ago, creates a fascinating yet somewhat eerie effect.

In the early 12th century, Gérard de Commarque donated his assets to the **Knights Templars**. The castle became a commandery which, following the tragic disappearance of the order, was passed over to the Hospitallers of Saint John of Jerusalem who built the enormous **dungeon**, then sold the place to the Baron of Beynac. Following the treaty of Brétigny (1360), the Sire of Commarque, like his cousin Beynac, joined Charles V and resisted the invading forces.

In 1370, Pons de Beynac died leaving Philippe, a **small girl of three years**, as his only successor. His heritage was threatened by his neighbour and rival, Castelnaud, who had followed the English camp. To guarantee its protection, **Pons de Commarque**, then in the prime of life, became engaged to the child. Fighting for France, he had become master over almost all of Black Périgord when he married Philippe in 1379; she was then aged 12. The young lady of Commarque was not to live long as, in 1405, Pons was remarried to Magne de Castelnaud.

In 1406, however, Commarque was beleaguered by the troops of Archambaud d'Abzac. Pons and his family remained prisoners of the English for six months, until their freedom was bought. As a reward for services rendered, Charles VII offered him Campagne castle. He died in 1440. His successors did not have his wisdom. Throughout the 15th and 16th centuries, they ravaged the surrounding countryside and held travellers to ransom, thus giving the castle its **dark reputation**.

Commarque: church ruins. In the background, Laussel Castle.

Commarque château and its high 13th century dungeon.

*Laussel viewed from Commarque.
Here, vegetable and mineral combine
in an extraordinary scene of genesis.*

The castle has today come back into the possession of the Commarque family and the owner, by undertaking to halt the decay of the building, has shown his desire to preserve the **wild, romantic character** of the site and leave access free to visitors. Having crossed the two drawbridges above the dry moats, protected by gatehouses, one discovers a main building constructed from the 13th to the 16th centuries, featuring transom windows and rugged-looking turret staircases. Strolling leisurely through the devastated rooms with their gaping fireplaces, the visitor may climb the huge **12th century square dungeon** to discover a staggering panorama, a landscape of genesis or apocalypse where the vegetable and mineral kingdoms seem to have conspired to exclude all human presence. At the foot of the castle,

*Puymartin Castle, near Sarlat.
It contains ancient furniture and 17th century
mural paintings. It is haunted by a White Lady.*

the mediaeval **village** where the Romanesque church and its crypt, and the bread oven of a collapsed house can be recognised.

Opposite stands **Laussel**, the elegant "little brother" of Beune valley — an essential complement to Commarque to capture the charm of the site. The **marsh plain**, formerly covered with hemp, spreads out between the two castles; today it conceals formidable muddy traps which are crossed by the clear stream of the Beune. The preserved landscape of time, of the darkest romanticism, could only be of inspiration to artistic minds. Robert Merle set the action to his book *Malevil* here, as did Claude Cénac for *Demain l'An Mil*. As for the film-maker, **Ridley Scott**, the end of his film *Duellistes* was shot here.

MARQUAY: CAP-BLANC and PUYMARTIN
(11 km N.W. of Sarlat)

Perched high on a hill between the two Beunes, the little village of Marquay groups its fine Périgord-style houses around its fortified **Romanesque church**, from the 12th and 13th centuries.

Five kilometres to the west, **Cap-Blanc** shelter offers an unforgettable **visit**. It conceals one of the most impressive prehistoric friezes known. Measuring 13 m in length, deep **sculptures of horses** and Bovidae which seem to spring out of the wall are waiting to be discovered. Their dimensions (the high-relief sculpture of the centre horse is 2.2 m long) and artistic

Cap-Blanc: sculpted horse.

Entrance to Bernifal cave.

Facing page: long before Man appeared, stalactites and stalagmites joined up to form columns in Proumeyssac chasm, near Le Bugue.

qualities give the frieze fascinating realism. These works date most probably back to the ancient or middle Magdalenian period (13,000 years B.C.).

Five kilometres to the west, above the Beune marshlands, opposite the formidable Commarque fortress, **Laussel castle**, from the 15th and 16th centuries, although greatly restored, has

Human representation known as "The Sorcerer" of Saint-Cirq du Bugue.

retained the elegant silhouette of its machicolated towers, its square dungeon and its 17th century chapel. Nearby, we find a curious **troglodytic dovecote** and the famous **prehistoric site** of **Laussel.**

Six kilometres to the south, near Sarlat, the elegant outline of **Puymartin** rises out of the forest. Built in the 15th and 16th centuries, and restored in the 19th century, it is **open to visitors** and houses an interesting collection of ancient furniture. It is said to be haunted by a "White Lady".

Near the village of **Meyrals**, one can visit **Bernifal** cave which features paintings and engravings from the Magdalenian period, and also the cave fort at **La Rhonie**.

LE BUGUE:
PROUMEYSSAC and BARA-BAHAU
(11 km to the west of Les Eyzies)

Surrounded by wooded hills, built in terraces on the right bank of a bend in the river Vézère, the welcoming **little town of Le Bugue** — the golden gate to prehistory — is, with its 3,000 inhabitants, one of the main localities in Black Périgord. A large, remarkably equipped **aquarium museum**, the "village of Le Bournat" (recreation of former trades), the museum of Palaeonthology and the wildlife house attract an increasing number of visitors.

One kilometre to the north-west, we find **Bara-Bahau cave**, discovered in 1951 by the speleologist Norbert Casteret. This 100 m long cavity is **open to the public**. In the soft, crumb-ly rock — Father Glory compared it to cream cheese — prehistoric artists engraved mysterious signs and outlines of aurochs, bears, bison, ibexes and horses with fingers, flint or sticks. The highly rustic style of these works make them difficult to date; they are probably from the ancient Magdalenian era (15,000 years B.C.).

Three kilometres to the south, **Proumeyssac chasm** is **open to visitors**. Here we discover a **limestone cavern** almost 50 metres high, a large number of translucent stalactites (which are still alive, thanks to a passing stream), "eccentrics" in weird forms, a petrifactive fountain and most strange triangular crystallisations. "**One of the finest showcases of underground France**", according to Norbert Casteret, Proumeyssac is a must for any visitor to the Périgord. With the remarkable efforts made by the owners to develop the site, we shall not miss the times when we descended the chasm, from the summit, in a fragile basket.

Four kilometres to the east, the little village of **Saint-Cirq du Bugue** has a **prehistoric cave open to visitors**, which features an exceptional **representation** of a full, human face. In addition to the prehistoric shelter, a visit may be made to the **cave fort** at Pech Saint-Sourd.

Near Le Bugue, we shall see **Campagne** castle (16th-18th centuries), the prehistoric site of **La Ferrassie** (Mousterian and Perigordian periods) and **Fleurac** castle, the birthplace of the Saint-Exupérys, and its motor vehicle museum. At the confluence of the Vézère and the Dordogne, the ancient village of **Limeuil** offers "the most splendid view over Périgord" according to Le Roy. You must also see the charming Saint-Martin's church, built by the King of England, for the atonement of the murder of the Archbishop of Canterbury, Thomas à Becket. You should also visit the strong, fortified **Paunat Abbey** (12th century), as well as the church (also fortified) and the vast lake at **Trémolat.**

Bara-Bohus: imprint of hand.

Le Bugue: the Golden Gate to Prehistory, general view.

Le Bugue and its splendid aquarium museum.

The land of the Bastides

Covered footpaths in Monpazier, 13th century English bastide.

Traditionally part of Purple Périgord (Périgord Pourpre),
the Land of the Bastides, between the Dordogne and the Dropt in the extreme south of the département,
even spills into Lot-et-Garonne. It owes its geographic unity to the vast Bessède forest which
was cleared and colonised in the 13th and 14th centuries, as new towns - the bastides - were founded.
Used as pretexts by the Sovereign to reduce feudal power and by the Church
to rid the region of Cathar "heresy", the bastides particularly marked the rivalry between the kings of France
and England, who were to find them a good reason to start the Hundred Years War.

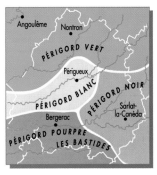

The lofty town of Belvès.

CADOUIN

(42 km S.W. of Sarlat)

Before leaving the Dordogne valley, we should make sure that we see **Saint-Cyprien** (12th, 14th and 16th century abbey church, 15th-17th century Château de La Roque and 16th-17th century Château de Fages), the tiny village of **Urval**, **Le Coux** church, the **Bigaroque** site, the ancient fortress of Pope Clement V and the lofty town of **Belvès**, the town of seven belfries, which is to open its underground passages to the public.

The village of **Cadouin**, with its old houses and market hall, has developed in the shadow of its **abbey.** This abbey was founded in 1115, in the heart of the deep Bessède forest, by Robert d'Arbrissel, prompted by Géraud de Sales. But the abbey's prosperity came from a prestigious relic brought from Antioch, of which traces are found in Cadouin as early as 1117 — the **Sindon** of Christ.

Hanging in a silver shrine in the church vault, it became the object of a important **pilgrimage** which brought together the humblest and the greatest. It is even said to have been visited by Eleanor of Aquitaine, Richard the Lionheart, Saint Louis, Blanche de Castille and Charles V. Prompted by Louis XI, reno-

vation work was carried out at the abbey, including the splendid **Gothic cloisters** which can still be seen today. Whilst the abbey was held in commendam, it experienced a decline from a spiritual aspect yet remained an active centre of pilgrimages. **Rabelais**, on a journey through Périgord, visited Cadouin and referred to the Sindon of Christ in *Gargantua*. The last monks were expelled during the Revolution. Pilgrimages started up again, however, in the 19th century; once again, the crowds flooded in to attend ceremonies and a lucrative trade in medallions, crosses and pious images was generated. The first doubts as to the authenticity of the Sindon were voiced in 1925 by Reverend Father Francez. An inquiry ordered in 1932 by the religious authorities revealed that this cloth, in spite of being of oriental origin, bore an 11th century Cufic inscription invoking the name of **Allah**. The Cadouin Sindon of Christ was an **imitation.**

The **Romanesque church** was consecrated in 1154. Its broad façade, divided into three sections by abutments, features a portal with triple arching surmounted by a row of blind arcades. Its austere appearance, typical of **Cistercian** churches, is tempered by the splendid Périgord golden stone and the sculptures on the external columns and the cornice modillions.

The Cistercian abbey in Cadouin. It has splendid Gothic-Renaissance cloisters.

Saint-Avit-Sénieur: the Romanesque abbey church fortified in the 14th century.

The interior includes three naves with barrel vaults, a pendentive-supported cupola and half-dome apsidioles.

Although damaged during the Wars of Religion and the Revolution, the Cadouin **cloisters**, with their richly decorated vaults and pillars, remain a **masterpiece of religious art**. Work began in the 15th century with the support of King Louis XI and were completed in the 16th century. The west gallery is decorated with remarkable Renaissance **sculptures**. Biblical themes (the tales of Job, Lazarus and Samson and Delilah) are combined with secular themes (satirical or popular scenes reminiscent of Flemish paintings and illustrations of fables). The vault features the Last Judgment, Abraham's sacrifice and the flight to Egypt. It also includes the remnants of 15th century frescos. Embedded in the stone in the north gallery, we find the monks' pews, the lector's seat and the abbot's seat which is surmounted on either side by two sculpted columns representing the ascent of Mount Calvary and a procession.

Between Cadouin and Beaumont, the tiny English *bastide* of **Molières**, the fortified church of **Saint-Avit-Sénieur** (11th and 14th centuries, museum) and the village of **Montferrand** (museum) must be visited.

Monpazier: Central square of Edward I, King of England's 13th century bastide.

pick with their neighbour Aymeric de Biron, Seigneur of Montferrand, of whom a number of serfs had taken flight, sought refuge in the bastide and obtained their freedom there as laid down in the charter. During the Hundred Years War, Monpazier changed hands several times. Following a century of calm, the area was ravaged by the Wars of Religion and, on 21st June 1574, the town was captured, through treachery, by the Huguenot captain, **Geoffroy de Vivans**. Monpazier was also the headquarters for the peasant revolutionaries, the *Croquants,* who held their assembly here on 22nd May 1594. Following several attacks on castles, the troubles calmed down in 1597. A new revolt in 1637 brought together *8000 Croquants* under the

orders of Buffarot, a weaver from the neighbouring village of Capdrot. Taken prisoner, **Buffarot** was quartered on 16th August 1637 in Monpazier main square. The first of June 1879 saw the birth in Monpazier of **Jean Galmont**, who became a journalist, writer, the author of two best sellers, *Quelle étrange histoire* and *Un mort vivait parmi nous,* and, above all, an adventurer. In *Rhum*, a book written by his friend, **Blaise Cendrars**, Monpazier was described as "an island of stones, very old stones… a geometric town like an American town".

Monpazier has retained its entire Gothic character. Still today, fairs are held on days laid down in the charter. The central square has kept its mediaeval appearance. It is surrounded

BEAUMONT-DU-PÉRIGORD
(29 km S.E. of Bergerac)

The *bastide* of Beaumont, founded in 1272, reigns peacefully today over a sleepy land. In the Middle Ages, however, it was one of the most important *bastides* in Périgord. The Seneschal of Guienne, Lucas de Thaney, presided over its creation on behalf of the King of England. Edward I, who called it his "premier Royal *bastide*", had it built not in a square, as was common practice, but, it is said, in the form of a letter H in memory of his father, Henry III. It was not fully "liberated from the English" until after the Battle of Castillon (1453). Beaumont has not retained as much of its original character as Domme or Monpazier, but the jewel in its crown is undoubtedly **Saint-Front church**, one of the finest **military gothic** churches in Périgord. This huge, austere construction was designed from the outset with a defensive purpose as, unlike most other *bastides*, Beaumont does not have a castle. The four towers joined by a parapet walk look more like dungeons than belfries. Yet the sculpted Gothic portal, surmounted by a balcony and a frieze of prominent figures, is quite elegant.

Beaumont: Luzier Gate, a vestige of 13th century fortifications.

Previous pages:
The military Gothic church in Beaumont-du-Périgord.

Near Beaumont, one can see the **Le Blanc covered passage**, fine **Bannes** castle, and, to the south of Bergerac, the walled town of **Issigeac**, which was dependent upon the bishopric of Sarlat, and the wonderful French bastide of **Eymet** (museum within the castle).

Beaumont: Saint-Front church, a fine example of military and religious architecture.

Top: Le Blanc covered passage, near the village of Nojals-et-Clotte.
Eymet Castle.

Bannes Castle.

MONPAZIER
(50 km S.W. of Sarlat)

Built overlooking the Dropt valley, **Monpazier** is certainly the finest and best preserved of Périgord's *English bastides*. Along with Beaumont, Molières, Lalinde and Fonroque, it formed part of the English defensive system to the south of the Périgord. Today, Monpazier still has a 400 m by 220 m North-South **grid layout**, surrounded by ramparts. The streets which cross at right-angles, are themselves intersected by a network of side streets. The **central square**, the courtyard of the bastide, is lined with **arcaded** houses.

Through an act of parliament dated 7th January 1284, **Edward I**, King of England and Duke of Aquitaine, decided to found the *bastide* of Monpazier. The foundation was carried out by **Jean de Grailly**, Seneschal of Périgord for Edward I who himself came to visit his *bastide* in 1286. The inhabitants enjoyed a number of benefits including tax relief and the abolition of seigneurial law. In spite of this, the foundation was laborious. The King had to lay down that any inhabitants who did abide by the obligation to build their house would be fined ten pounds. The consuls, elected to run the town, also had a bone to

Monpazier: Central square of Edward I, King of England's 13th century bastide.

pick with their neighbour Aymeric de Biron, Seigneur of Montferrand, of whom a number of serfs had taken flight, sought refuge in the bastide and obtained their freedom there as laid down in the charter. During the Hundred Years War, Monpazier changed hands several times. Following a century of calm, the area was ravaged by the Wars of Religion and, on 21st June 1574, the town was captured, through treachery, by the Huguenot captain, **Geoffroy de Vivans**. Monpazier was also the headquarters for the peasant revolutionaries, the *Croquants,* who held their assembly here on 22nd May 1594. Following several attacks on castles, the troubles calmed down in 1597. A new revolt in 1637 brought together ***8000 Croquants*** under the

orders of Buffarot, a weaver from the neighbouring village of Capdrot. Taken prisoner, **Buffarot** was quartered on 16th August 1637 in Monpazier main square. The first of June 1879 saw the birth in Monpazier of **Jean Galmont**, who became a journalist, writer, the author of two best sellers, *Quelle étrange histoire* and *Un mort vivait parmi nous*, and, above all, an adventurer. In *Rhum*, a book written by his friend, **Blaise Cendrars**, Monpazier was described as "an island of stones, very old stones… a geometric town like an American town".

Monpazier has retained its entire Gothic character. Still today, fairs are held on days laid down in the charter. The central square has kept its mediaeval appearance. It is surrounded

Monpazier market.

church, built in the 13th and 14th centuries, features a façade restored around 1550. In the chancel, fine stalls dating back to 1492 are sculpted with fantastic or grotesque figures.

BIRON
(58 km S.E. of Sarlat)

Seven kilometres to the south-west of the splendid *bastide* of Monpazier, at the border between Périgord and the Agen region, reigns the **largest castle** in Dordogne. The enormous mass of this **barony** of Périgord looks out over a distance of 30 km in all directions. A rare, if not unique specimen, the fief belonged to the Gontaut family for twenty-four generations, from the 12th century to 1938. This perenniality helped to fashion a harmonious architectural *ensemble* in spite of the differing styles and the turbulent events of history. In 1189, Gaston de Gontaut married his daughter Raymonde to the **Cathar**, **Martin d'Algais**, Sire of Bigaroque and Seneschal of Gascony and Périgord for the King of England. The crusade having put the south-west to fire and sword, the Cathar forces shut themselves inside Biron in 1211 where they were besieged by Simon de Montfort. In return for their lives, he got the defenders to hand over Martin d'Algais. D'Algais was dragged behind a horse before being hung.

Biron: the castle dominates the village
where Bernard Palissy is said to have lived.

by arcades also known as *cornières* (roof valleys) or *couverts* (covered footpaths), as they form a covered gallery. The houses surrounding the square are all of the same size, 8 m wide by 20 m deep, and are separated by alleys which acted as a firebreak and a garbage dump. In the square, the 16th century **market halls** have preserved their old corn measures. A well is to be found in one corner. The city walls still have **three fortified gates** out of the original six — one to the south and two to the north. These two are surmounted by circular towers. A postern, the "gateway to Heaven", opens up to the west. Near the church, the 13th-14th century Chapter house, a former tithe-collector's barn, has gemel bay windows over its three floors. The **Gothic**

The descendants of the illustrious Gontaut family continued to survive throughout the Wars of Religion. They remained Catholic, yet received the Queen of Navarre and the Prince of Condé. **Armand de Gontaut-Biron**, a companion of Henry IV and field-marshal in 1576, fought at Evry and Arques before being killed during the siege of Épernay in 1592. Brantôme, a good judge of men of arms, had named him "France's greatest captain".

His son, **Charles de Gontaut** (1562-1602), had inherited his fiery temperament. Henry IV, who adored him, called him "the sharpest instrument of his victories". The King laden the young man with honours, making him an admiral, a field-marshal in 1595, a lieutenant-general of the armed forces, a duke and peer in 1598, and the Governor of Burgundy. But his ambition destroyed him. With the Duke of Savoy and the Spanish Governor of Milan, he conspired to dismember the kingdom which would leave him Aquitaine. The King pardoned him. He hatched yet another plot and stirred up trouble. The King would have pardoned him yet again in return for a full confession, but he refused. He was beheaded on 31st July 1602 at the Bastille. The King regretted parting company with the one who, in his own words, could "no more prevent himself from speaking ill of others than from doing good when he [had] his backside in the saddle and a sword in his hand".

Property of the *département* of Dordogne since 1978, Biron is **open to the public**. It is not a castle which you are going to visit, but a group of castles from different epochs which are as difficult to take in visually as it is to imagine. No description can accurately render the image of this jumble of architecture and sculptures. Jean Secret distinguished three groups.

One enters the castle through a square tower, the base of which dates back to the 13th century, but which was reworked in the 15th and 16th centuries. The gatehouse, which has an elabo-rate gate and gable window, provides access to an initial courtyard. Next to the entrance tower, a Renaissance **loggia** leads us to the **collegial chapel**. This is the finest "room" in the castle. This two-storey section has two naves, one above the other. The ground floor looks out on to the village and is used as a parish church. The first floor which opens out on to the castle is the seigneurial chapel. With its ribbed vaults, it combines harmoniously the flamboyant Gothic and Renaissance styles. It contains richly sculpted tombs with **recumbent figures** of the builders of the chapel and restorers of the castle — Pons de Gontaut, who died in 1524, and his brother, Bishop of Sarlat, who died in 1531.

Isolated to the north of this low courtyard, a small 14th century **manor house** whose vaults are decorated with 16th century frescos, was formerly the collector's office where peasant's came to pay their tithe. Symmetrically opposite this building, and dating back to the same epoch, we find a round tower, the *tour Saint-Pierre*.

A Louis XIV staircase and a Renaissance portal leads to the **main courtyard** where the antique 12th century **dungeon** has an imposing presence. A group of buildings from the Renaissance and Louis XIV periods, including the States General room, built in the early 17th century by the Marshal of Biron, is slightly overwhelming by its mass. At the back of the courtyard, a **peristyle** with fine 17th century columns provides a pleasant panoramic view of the countryside. The visit ends with the marshals' pavilion and the immense kitchens in the base of the castle. The castle acts as a venue for exhibitions of plastic arts during the summer, and as a setting for films. On the road back to Sarlat, one should visit the *bastide* of **Villefranche-du-Périgord** (mushroom and chestnut museum), and the Romanesque church in Besse, with its sculpted portal.

Biron castle is the largest in the Périgord.

White Périgord

Saint-Frontchurch in Périgueux.

In the heart of the region,
the Isle valley marks out a quite heavily urbanised area with,
in the centre, Périgueux, its two thousand-year-old capital.
This is White Périgord (Périgord Blanc), an old land where the Romans left their mark.
To get the full taste of its charm, why not leave the towns and main roads.

HAUTEFORT

(30 km to the north of Montignac)

Hautefort Castle can be spotted from afar. Its "Louis XIV" style comes as quite a surprise in our region. Perched on a hill, it combines the haughty position of Middle Age fortresses and the perfect equilibrium of 17th century constructions.

Having crossed the drawbridge, we enter the castle through a gatehouse flanked by two watch towers, dating back to 1588. We then discover a large main building, preceded by two wings, ending in two round **towers** topped with **pinnacle turrets**. The main section, flanked by two domed pavilions, is surrounded by two further pavilions dating back to the 18th century. The perfect **symmetry** of the building is reinforced by the harmonious, well balanced slate roofing. A grand staircase leads down from the first to the ground floor. This includes a splendid balcony with basket-handle arches. The interior of the castle has a rich selection of **furniture**. In the west tower, with its fine structural work, a number of craft objects are waiting to be discovered, in addition to an evocation of the works of **Eugène Le Roy**, born in the castle in 1836. But the most stunning treasure at Hautefort is possibly its 30,000 m² of **grounds** with its wide variety of trees and its **ornamental gardens** with its rich combination of flower beds, hedges of box-trees and covered passages of conifers. An extreme sense of pleasure is to be felt by walking through the gardens in search of the shadows of the famous people who lived here.

Along with his contemporary, Bernard de Ventadour, **Bertran de Born** (1150-1214) is the most famous of all Occitan **troubadours**. He most certainly sang of women and life in the seigneurial courts, but let's not imagine him with a love-struck eye and his lute under his arm. If, like all good troubadours, he travelled from castle to castle, it was to take them by storm because de Born was above all a formidable warlord, a **"spreader of discord"**. These words of Dante, which precipitated the poet into the hell of the "Divine comédie", sums him up marvellously. Having stripped his brother of his share of inheritance, he got involved in the quarrels of the Plantagenets. His castle was besieged five times. An opponent of Richard the Lionheart, he pushed his brother Henri le Court-Mantel to revolt against his father, Henry II, the King of England. His hopes collapsed with the sudden death of Henri le Court-Mantel. Worn out by a hectic life, Bertran de Born retired in 1196 to the neighbouring **Le Dalon Abbey** where he died around 1214. Remains of Le Dalon Abbey which, along with Cluny, was the largest church of Christendom, are still to be found at Sainte-Trie.

Hautefort Castle preserves the memory of Marie de Hautefort, the favourite of Louis XIII.

Hautefort and its ornamental gardens.

Hautefort: Inside the castle.

Facing page, top left: Structural work in the south-west tower.

Facing page, top right: Hautefort, from the troubadour Bertran de Born, to Marie, the "Aurora" of Louis XIII.

Facing page, bottom: Hautefort, ornamental gardens.

The Marquis **Jean-François**, born in 1610, who distinguished himself at the battle of Rocroi (1643), gave Hautefort its present-day appearance. He was reputed to be avaricious and it is said that Molière used him as a model for his **Harpagnon**. The Marquise de Sévigné thus said of his death in 1680, "He refused to take any English remedies, saying that they were too costly. We told him, 'Sire, you will give but forty pistoles'. His last words were 'It's too much'".

The fate of his sister, **Marie d'Hautefort** (1616-91), was somewhat out of the ordinary. Born at the castle, Marie became maid of honour to Maria de Medici when she was but twelve years of age. She soon caught the eye of King **Louis XIII**, and the rest of the court. Her beauty and charms, as well as her modesty, piety and virtue, inspired real passion in the King at which **Anne of Austria** took no umbrage at all. This young blonde from Périgord, nicknamed **Aurora** for her beauty, was

she not finally to waken the senses of her royal spouse? She was wrong. The relationship between Louis and Marie was, and remained, a platonic one. **Richelieu** attempted to get her to spy on the Queen, yet she refused — an act which was to make her the enemy of the Cardinal. Richelieu finally managed to separate the King from his favourite by serving up a new mistress, Mademoiselle de La Fayette. Marie wisely waited for this romance to end to win back the King's heart. She succeeded, but her return to favour did not last long. Pressed by the Cardinal and undoubtedly weary of the fits of temper and the haughty reproaches of Marie, Louis XIII exiled her. She only returned to Paris after the deaths of the Cardinal and the King in 1643. Becoming once again, at the age of 27, the darling of the court, she took the liberty of rejecting the most attractive marriage proposals. Her incessant affairs ended up alienating the Queen's good graces from her. Dismissed once again, she en-

*Above: Excideuil. The castle
has two huge square dungeons
from the 12th century, linked by a
14th and 15th century building.*

*Right: Savignac-Lédrier, an industrial
world in a rural environment. From 1421 to 1930,
the Périgord forges produced
up to 10% of the kingdom's iron.*

tered a convent in 1644 only to come out two years later to
marry, at the age of 30, the Marshal of Schomberg, Duke of
Halluin. Widowed at the age of 40, she devoted herself henceforth to charity work. The one whom her contemporaries referred to as **"the mother of the poor"** died at the age of 75,
having restored her good name.

To the west of Hautefort, one should visit **Tourtoirac**
(Romanesque abbey), where the memory of Antoine de
Tounens, King of Patagonia and Araucania, lingers and the little
town of **Excideuil** (castle and church).

To the north, on the Auvézère, **Savignac-Lédrier forge**,
open to visitors, preserves the memory of a period when
Périgord produced 10 % of the kingdom's iron. Above, one
finds the Renaissance château of the forgemaster. To the south
of Hautefort, we can see **Badefols d'Ans** Castle (14th and 15th
centuries) and the ruins of the legendary **Muratel** fortress.

PÉRIGUEUX

Although Périgueux is the main administrative town in the *département* of Dordogne (it has a population of 60,000), it still has little industry. We should however mention the stamp factory, the only one in France. A very active town from a cultural point of view, Périgueux offers visitors exhibitions, concerts and drama productions all year round, and, in the summer, a **mime festival**.

**In search of Gallo-Roman
and Early Mediaeval Antiquity
– The "City" of Vésone**

We really ought to begin our visit by the City church from where we descend towards **Vésone Tower** via Rue Romaine. Once facing the tower, our attention will firstly be drawn to the background formed by the hills of La Boissière and **Ecornebeuf** — it is here, indeed, that tradition situates the

Périgueux: the Roman Vésone Tower, the remains of a huge temple.

The old quarters of Périgueux combine the traditional with the modern.

Facing page: On the bank of the Isle, Saint-Front Cathedral, restored in the 19th century.

Overleaf: The roofs of Saint-Front Cathedral.

Périgueux museum: bifaces.

birthplace of the town, the capital of the City of the Petrocores. The powerful building which stands before us (almost thirty metres tall with an outside diameter of twenty metres) is, in fact, only the most sacred part (the **cella**) of a temple of a much greater size. Bonded with ashlar, the enclosure is decorated with chains of brickwork above which the presence of cavities will be noted. Beams supporting a peristyle were wedged into these cavities. As for the outside wall, still visible a few paces further on, it stretches some 140 metres along its main side, testifying to the size of the building, probably built in the first century and altered several times since. ***The domus des bouquets***, in the apparent disorder of the excavations which have revealed elements dating back to various periods (including, right next to the fence, elements of an Augustan residence), features a group of buildings from the second century including those identified as the atrium, a hypocaust, etc.

Continuing their stroll, having traversed the administrative sector (the main building of which is the seminary built in the 18th century), visitors will not fail to be surprised by the monumental wall which they will discover on crossing the iron railway bridge. Passing in front of **Barrière Castle**, without stopping for the moment, one reaches the Romanesque gate known as the **Porte Normande**. At the foot of this gate, an inextricable tangle of capital-headed column shafts and sculpted blocks may lead one for a moment to believe the legend that an enclosure was built in extreme haste during the third century as the sound of hooves could be heard coming from the horses of the invader, Alaman. Skirting round this chaotic sight, one reaches the other face of the wall. The strong, regular bonding proves that this ensemble clearly belonged to a project which had come down from above and long matured. The Romanesque house (on the left) and the dungeon of Barrière Castle were built in the Middle Ages on Roman foundations. The castle belonged to

those families of local aristocracy who, after the fifth century, along with the bishop's people, held the **Christian city** enclosed inside its walls. The villagers from the surrounding flat

Facing page: The Chapter mill reflecting in the Isle.

The ruins of Barrière Castle (Top and bottom photos).

lands came to take refuge here whenever there was a risk of invasion. Returning from the bridge, one should not fail to enter the castle grounds which feature a range of structures from classical mediaeval (13th century dungeon) to Renaissance (16th century polygonal tower). Due attention should also be paid to the fine **flamboyant style gate**.

How important was Vesunna in her days of glory? The yardstick which we often tend to use to measure this is the capacity of public buildings. The largest in this respect is surely what the locals call **"les arènes"** — the first century **amphitheatre.** This edifice which, it is estimated, could contain as many as 20,000 people, was built on the model of the Rome Coliseum. The amphitheatre, initially an essential part of the third century wall, was converted into a fortress (La Rolphie Castle) by the Counts of Périgord who, during the Hundred Years War, had become pillaging barons who were not averse to a few dirty deeds. It failed to survive the downfall of these extremely sad specimens, of whom the most famous, Archambaud, gave himself to the English. The fortress was consequently dismantled on Royal orders at the end of the 14th century.

The visit to the **City** will end with its **church.** No-one better than Jean Secret has been able to describe the sober elegance of

cupolas, the remnants of an initial construction of which there were four up to the Wars of Religion. And these two cupolas, one from the late 11th and the other from the mid-12th century, provide an illustration of how, in this architectural part of the region, Périgord has successfully won recognition and how it has gradually been able to overcome heaviness and, through the use of increasingly slender pediments, resolve the famous problem of "squaring the circle" — a square floor surface and a domed roof — making the church the symbol of the passage from earth to heaven at the same time as a place of salvation.

Le Puy-Saint-Front

Leaving the City, we just have to walk around the building to notice **Mataguerre Tower**. It is at the foot of this tower that we shall begin our visit to the second hub around which the town was built - Le Puy-Saint-Front.

Dating back to the 14th century, Mataguerre Tower appears to be the only significant vestige of the vast enclosure which surrounded Le Puy-Saint-Front from the 12th century. The term **"Puy-Saint-Front"** designates in fact the small town which

The 14th century Mataguerre Tower, the only remains of the ramparts which encircled Le Puy-Saint-Front.

grew around the hillock overlooking the river Isle and where the tomb of the Apostle of Périgord was supposed to be found. It is probably in connection with the commercial revival in the 11th century and the development of pilgrimages (Le Puy-Saint-Front became an important stage on the road to Compostela), that activity started up again here. The inhabitants of this market town soon had a bone to pick with the lay or ecclesiastic aristocracy of the City whose guardianship they naturally found difficult to support. In the late 13th century, through the voice of Louis IX, the monarchic authority united the two rivals and put an end to the clashes of which Place Francheville (known as l'Entre-Deux-Villes, *Inter-Town*) was often the venue. This small town grew remarkably up to the 14th century. To set the scene, you just need to take the side streets rising up to the cathedral, like Rue des Farges, to imagine the day-to-day life in an extremely densely populated town. No fewer than 2500 homes, or more than 10,000 inhabitants, lived in a space representing one-sixth of the town's current surface area.

From **Place Hoche**, visitors will be pleased to continue their medieval promenade via **Rue du Calvaire** where they will be able to admire, amongst other things, the seventh century **Provost's House** (*Maison du Viguier*), the present-day Saint-Front school, behind its studded door. This street leads to **Place de la Clautre**, the site of the most controversial monument in the whole region — **Saint-Front Cathedral**. Cathedral or Cathedrals, because the part of the building which can be seen on leaving Rue du Calvaire has a twin peculiarity. Firstly it is the oldest because construction began in the late tenth century, at the time of Bishop Frotaire, and secondly, its façade includes re-used elements originating from classical antiquity and the Merovingian period. Today, this coverless ensemble forms an open courtyard where everything points to the fact that one had planned to mount a cupola. This stands in front of, and is attached to, a **belfry**. Almost all of this 60-metre belfry is also as how it was built back in the 12th century. This is not at all the case for the second church, the cathedral itself. Here we discover an edifice built to a cruciform design as was delivered to us by what we must call the reconstruction of the 19th century.

Inside the building, we might forget the relative coldness of the whole by admiring the purity of the lines of the double cupolas. Neither shall we remain insensitive to the fine reredos illustrating the Assumption of Virgin Mary. We might also ask to see the cloisters around which guided **visits** are organised during the

The City church.

tourist season. In Rue Saint-Front, visitors will surely notice a strange 19th century building whose façade is sculpted with symbols - it is one of the finest **Masonic temples** in France.

Leaving the cathedral, one must go down towards the river. To the left, the recently restored **Chapter mill** provides evidence of the site of the former mill-course which started at Tournepiche Bridge, today known as Barris Bridge. Having crossed this bridge, we come across two fine manors forming what is traditionally called in Périgueux **"la Maison des Consuls"** (*the Consuls'House*), but which have nothing to do with municipal institutions. **Cayla House** is reminiscent of the houses in Rue Aubergerie by copying their archaic mediaeval structures, mixing them with a hint of the flamboyant style in the decoration of the gable windows. To the left, on the other hand, the rather febrile grace of the colonnettes of **Lambert House** takes us back to the time of Francis I and the Italian Wars.

We then need to cross the road, proceed a short way and take **Rue du Port-de-Graule** off to the left. We shall stop at the entrance to this street to take in the view of this fine old example of popular Périgueux. At the end of the street, a series of alleys is of obvious interest. Taking the flight of steps, we reach **Avenue Daumesnil**, before going off immediately to the left along **Rue du Plantier**, then back down **Rue Notre-Dame, Rue des Francs-Maçons, Rue de la Constitution** and, finally, **Rue de la Nation**. But it is undoubtedly in the central part of Le Puy-Saint-Front, around **Rue Limogeanne**, where we discover the finest creations and where work carried out over the last ten years has given its hallmark back to the town. We are advised to take **Rue de la Clarté** where we shall see, on the right, a fine 18th century house which was the birthplace of the man who remained known

for his famous reproach, General Daumesnil. From here, we shall take **Rue Salinière**, then **Rue du Serment** which will bring us out on to the **Place de l'Hôtel de Ville**. Here lived the rival of Voltaire, **Lagrange-Chancel,** whose epigrams against the *Dauphin* were well known in the Age of Enlightenment. On this square, at n° 7, a **15th century building** offers visitors the grace of a polygon turret staircase. We then enter the main thoroughfare of local trade, the buzzing **Rue Limogeanne**. It features a series of fine manors of which **Estignard House** is the jewel in the crown. To get there, it is still best to take the alley immediately off to the right which leads to two charming little squares in an Italianist style and then on to **Rue de la Miséricorde**. This provides an excellent point from which to view **Estignard House** and its transom gable windows framed with stone hounds.

We shall end our tour with two museums. The *Musée du Périgord*, situated on the edge of Allées Tourny, has remarkable **prehistoric collections** and a large section devoted to Gallo-Roman antiques. The **military museum** is to be found in Rue des Forges.

Upstream of Périgueux, we shall visit the 16th century **Château des Bories** on the bank of the Isle and, on the Auvézère, the site of **Auberoche Fortress**, razed during the Hundred Years War.

Chancelade and the Isle Valley

To the north of Périgueux, we shall pay a visit to the Romanesque **Chancelade Abbey**, founded around 1125 by the hermit, Foucault. It was rebuilt in the 17th century by the blessed **Alain de Solminhac**. An abbey church, monastery buildings, the abbot's house and Saint-Jean chapel form a most

The Château des Bories, built between 1497 and 1604.

Château-l'Évêque. Saint Vincent de Paul
was ordained priest here in 1600.

Saint-Astier, on the banks of the Isle,
has preserved some fine Renaissance residences.

Top photo: Chancelade. The abbey had a broad cultural influence in the 17th century.
Lagrange-Chancel took refuge here to write his "Philippiques" against the regent, Philippe d'Orléans.

interesting group. A few kilometres away, a visit must be paid to **Merlande Priory (open to visitors)**, isolated in its vale. Its fortified chapel features a number of remarkable Romanesque sculptures. Further north, the castle at **Château-l'Évêque** was used as a residence by the bishops of Périgueux. **Saint Vincent de Paul** was ordained priest here.

Going back down the Isle Valley, to the west of Périgueux, we shall discover the fortified church of **Saint-Astier** (visits to the belfry and the crypt) and several châteaux, open to visitors. The Renaissance **Château de Neuvic** has a beautiful garden, while the **Château des Frateaux** features an underground passage and a pottery museum. To the south, the **Forteresse de Grignols** (12th to 17th century), which once belonged to the Talleyrands, has been refurnished. In Issac, we shall visit the 16th century **Château**

Top: The Renaissance Château de Neuvic. Inside, Louis XVI drawing room and 17th and 18th century frescos.

Above left: the Forteresse de Grignols with its 14th century dungeon. The Renaissance dining room has a Gothic fireplace blazoned with the Talleyrand coat of arms.

Above right: Château de Montréal. Its seigneur, Claude de Pontbriand, is said to have given its name to the Canadian city.

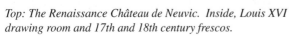

Right: Merlande Priory..

de Montréal which gave the city in Quebec its name. The chapel houses a number of recumbent figures, the statues of the twelve Apostles and a reliquary of the Holy Thorn, found on the body of Lord Talbot on the night of the Battle of Castillon. In **Mussidan**, the museum of art and popular traditions must be seen.

Green Périgord

Saint-Jean-de-Côle.

The north of the region, Green Périgord (Périgord Vert), lives under a twin influence.
The eastern half, around Hautefort, Thiviers and Jumilhac, features the Limousin province.
The western half, between Brantôme and Ribérac, is entirely turned towards the Angoumois.
Nontron, the capital, is right in the middle. With the valleys of the Bandiat-Tardoire,
and particularly the line formed by the river Côle and the river Dronne,
Green Périgord is a splendid area for tourism, still largely unknown.

JUMILHAC-LE-GRAND
(49 km east of Nontron)

At the northern edge of Green Périgord, bordering the Limousin, in a green undulating setting, the **Château de Jumilhac** looks out from its cliff over the waters of the Isle, which is still but a stream flowing in the bottom of the gorge. In 1579, a rich farmer and forgemaster, **Antoine Chapelle**, married the heiress to the estate. Made wealthy by the iron trade, Chapelle was able to finance the campaigns of the future Henry IV. To thank him, the King visited him at the Château de Jumilhac and ennobled him in 1597.

This newly created member of the nobility then had the current château built in place of the 13th-14th century fortress. The Gothic style of the building was a little outdated for the epoch which preferred airier buildings. The château, which is **open to visitors**, has a fairy-tale outline with its pointed towers and roofs. The building of red crystalline schist seems to have been

The château at Jumilhac-le-Grand.
Louise d'Hautefort was held prisoner here for twenty years.

Jumilhac, the roofing has been described as "the most romantic in France" (rear view).

Varaignes - the castle restored by the inhabitants of the village contains a fascinating museum of country life in the 19th and 20th centuries.

Mareuil Castle saw the birth of the troubadour, Arnaud de Mareuil.

constructed to no specific plan, more so for the decor than for the dwelling. The main building has Renaissance windows and bartizans. The **roofing**, described as "the most **romantic** in France", by Gustave Doré, has watch turrets and chimneys arranged around the "marquis's hat" which caps a tall tower. Among the figures represented along the lead ridge finials, we find birds, angels and various eminent people. The history of Jumilhac is retraced in a room by the entrance. On the second floor, a small room with semicircular arches and walls decorated with naive frescos is furnished with a bed and spinning wheel. The door is decorated with a **portrait** known as **"La Fileuse"** (The Spinner), the work of an unknown artist. This is the portrait of Louise d'Hautefort, held as a prisoner for twenty years by her husband, Antoine II de Jumilhac, son of Antoine Chapelle. In the village, we find a **gold museum** (Mine aux Fouilloux).

NONTRON and MAREUIL

From east to west, the northern fringe of Périgord has a number of points of interest. **Nontron** has an antique doll and

The restored Mareuil Castle has some interesting collections.

Facing page, top left: The portal of the Romanesque Bussière-Badil church with its triple arch and sculpted archstones.
Facing page, top right: Château de la Marthonie, Saint-Jean-de-Côle.
Facing page, bottom: The Gothic bridge in Saint-Jean-de-Côle.

toy museum. In **Teyjat,** we shall visit the Mège shelter and the **Town Hall Cave** (*Grotte de la Mairie*) with its Magdalenian carvings. In **Varaignes**, famous for its turkey fair, the 13th-16th century castle houses the Museum of the Bandiat-Tardoire Valleys (country life). In the far north, we shall see **Bussière-Badil** church with its remarkable sculptures, **Piégut** dungeon and the site of **Le Roc Branlant**, in Saint-Estèphe. To the south-west of Nontron, **Mareuil Castle**, one of the four baronies of Périgord, is **open to visitors**. Among its remnants from the 15th and 17th centuries, we shall come across the memory of the troubadour, Arnaud de Mareuil. To the south, the **Château des Bernardières** (12th-17th century) is **open to visitors**.

SAINT-JEAN-DE-CÔLE, THIVIERS and SORGES
(20 km N.E. of Brantôme)

Saint-Jean-de-Côle is a charming little **village** which lies by the Côle, a fresh, lively river with a number of small waterfalls and straddled by an old Gothic humpbacked bridge with starlings. The Périgord-style houses roofed in brown tiles earned the village the title of the **"finest roofs in France"**. The main square is closed to the right by the **Château de la Marthonie** and, at the back, by the vast **church** and the **priory** which is preceded by a **market hall** with remarkable structural work. The church and Augustinian priory were erected between 1086 and 1099 by the Bishop of Périgueux, Renaud de Thiviers. The design of the beautiful **church** of grey granite roofed with tiles is unique in Périgord. The huge square **nave** with a single, very high, bay is crowned with a **cupola** measuring 12.6 m in diameter — the largest in the region. The flattened dome section having collapsed on a number of occasions through the centuries, it is now replaced by flooring. The nave ends in a pentagonal apse and two radiant chapels of the same size. The interior combines the discreetness of Romanesque architecture and **Louis XIV** decor. On the outside, in addition to the weighty rectangular two-storey belfry from the 17th century, our attention will be drawn to the apse and chapel, decorated with applied arches extending into abutment columns whose **sculpted**

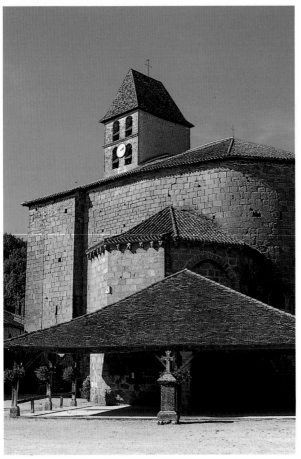

The market hall and square-nave church in Saint-Jean-de-Côle.

Agonac: The fortified Romanesque church.

Top: The impressive ruins
of Bruzac Castle.

capitals represent biblical scenes — Daniel and the lions, God modelling the face of Adam, angels, the intoxication of Noah and the Annunciation. Beneath the roof of the three chapels, some **75 sculpted modillions** of masks, monsters, wrestlers, obscene characters and animals are to be discovered.

Besides its church, Saint-Jean-de-Côle **priory** has preserved a 17th century **vestry** and a **library** in which the ceiling, painted by Lesueur, features an inset of the "ravishing of Saint Paul" attributed to Lebrun. Finally, our attention will be drawn to the prior's house, the two sides of the two-storey Renaissance **cloisters** and the abbey mill which was formerly powered by the waters of the Côle. Next to the abbey, the 15th and 17th century **Château de la Marthonie** is **open to visitors**.

To the south, we shall visit the splendid ruins of **Bruzac Castle** (13th-16th century). In **Thiviers**, where **Jean-Paul Sartre** spent his childhood, we shall see the old town and the museum devoted to **foie gras**. Further to the south, the mediaeval **Corgnac** bridge and 16th and 17th century **Laxion Castle** will attract the traveller. In **Sorges**, we shall visit the **truffle** eco-museum and the 15th century **Jaillac Castle**. Near **Agonac**, where we shall see a fine Romanesque church, the **Ligueux** Benedictine abbey, founded around 1115 by Géraud de Sales, is **open to visitors**.

VILLARS: PUYGUILHEM and BOSCHAUD
(12 km N.E. of Brantôme)

Villars might justifiably be named "the village of the three wonders".

One kilometre to the north, the architecture of the extremely elegant **Château de Puyguilhem** is reminiscent of the harmony of the châteaux of the Loire Valley. This "Azay-le-Rideau" lost in the Périgord is **open to visitors**. The current château was erected in the 16th century, most probably by **Mandot de la Marthonie**, and completed by his brothers, Jean and Gaston, Bishops of Dax from 1514 to 1555. Mandot, born in 1466, President of the Bordeaux Parliament, and later of the Paris Parliament, was charged with the running of the kingdom by Francis I after his departure for Italy. He died in Blois in 1517.

Château de Puyguilhem, Villars. An "Azay-le-Rideau" lost in Périgord.

Overleaf: Brantôme Abbey and the old stone bridge of 1538.

Standing at the end of a tree-lined drive in a rural setting, Puyguilhem is composed of a large main building with, to the right, a large **round tower** on to which an octagonal turret staircase has been built, and, to the left, a pentagonal tower with a pyramid roof. Two wings of unequal length complete the rear of the house. The north wing, built on to the round tower, is from the Renaissance period whereas the south wing dates back to the 18th century. The façade of the main house is decorated with transom windows, an open-work balustrade surmounted by **three beautiful gable windows**, and an elegant roof with a magnificent sculpted chimney stack. The turret staircase, like the preceding tower, is decorated in a Louis XII style. Beneath the windows, we discover **large sculpted panels** of letters in a rich decor of pearls, cords, chains and crowns. Beneath the roof, a band reveals a whole series of letters put together, it would seem, according to a secret code. At the other end of the façade, the main staircase is housed in a pentagonal tower from the Francis I period. The **capitals** of the doorway feature human masks, and the lintel, a chalice held by two Cupids. The visit indoors begins with the guard room in the round tower, the walls of which are pierced with loopholes and the fireplace sculpted with medallions. The kitchen has kept its utensils and a large table. Passing through the dining room, we enter a large room with fine ornate fireplace. The **furniture** includes a Flemish buffet of sculpted oak, a Spanish chest and an Aubusson tapestry. We then go up a remarkable **grand staircase** of which the splendid coffered ceiling features hanging keystones and bases sculpted with letters, the ribs extending towards sculptures of animals (bulls, lions etc.) and plants. On the first floor, one room features a most rare object, a vast **fireplace** of which the niched mantelpiece is decorated with six of the twelve Herculean tasks — a real work of art. On the second floor, one can admire the chestnut structural work in the form of an upturned hull. The château provides a home for prestigious collections every summer.

One kilometre to the west, Boschaud Abbey, founded in 1154, one of the four **Cistercian** abbeys in Périgord with Peyrouze, Cadouin and Le Dalon, may be **visited.** Boschaud is a unique example of a Cistercian abbey whose church comprises a line of **cupolas.** Today in ruins, the church with a triple-

bay nave was surmounted by three or four fine cupolas. The chancel still exists, as does a part of the transept whose cupola has been remounted. Flanked by two semi-circular apses, the half-dome apse has three bay windows, one of which is decorated with colonnettes. Boschaud has retained a part of its abbey buildings (a chapter house with ogival windows, a Romanesque vestry and the remains of the cloisters, dorter and apartments) and the outer enclosure.

Four kilometres to the north-east, **Villars** (or Cluzeau) **cave**, with its rich concretions, is **open to visitors**. In addition to its remarkable **formations**, it features around thirty **paintings** and carvings dating back 15,000-17,000 years. The long access road is marked with a dotted line of red and black ochre. The most interesting figures include the famous **"Blue horse"** and, at the back of the cave, as at Lascaux, the drawing of a man attacked by a bison. During our trip around the special visitors section, we shall discover a real **underground fairyland** — pools, block fields, eccentric formations, cascades,

candles, ceilings of stalactites and drapes — over several hundred metres. The cave also shows very clear signs of having been occupied by bears.

To the south, we shall visit the castle at **La Chapelle-Faucher** (15th and 17th centuries). During the Wars of Religion, in 1569, Admiral de Coligny massacred 260 peasants who had taken refuge here.

BRANTÔME
(27 km north of Périgueux)

Surrounded by a loop in the river Dronne, the little town of Brantôme (2000 inhabitants) is referred to as **"the Venice of Périgord"**.

In the early Christian era, a community is said to have lived in the **underground shelters** of La Fontaine-du-Rocher, and Saint Front is said to have destroyed a statue of Mercury here.

Facing page, top: Sculpted gable windows of the Château de Puyguilhem.

Facing page, bottom: Ruins of the Cistercian abbey in Boschaud.

On the banks of the Dronne, Brantôme and its belfry from the Carolingian period.

The circular dungeon of Piégut-Pluviers, the remains of a 12th century fortress destroyed by Richard the Lionheart.

Facing page, top: Brantôme. Behind the abbey, the cave of "the last judgment" and its 15th and 17th century sculptures.

Facing page, bottom: Ruins of La Chapelle-Faucher castle. Here, Admiral de Coligny massacred 260 peasants who had taken refuge here in 1569.

The town's pride is its **Benedictine abbey** which dates back to 769 or 786. Charlemagne is said to have donated to the brand new monastery, relics of Saint Sicaire, one of the victims of the massacre of the Holy Innocent. Devastated by the Vikings a few years later, it was rebuilt towards the end of the tenth century. The town and the abbey developed thereafter. It was here that Du Guesclin, who had come to see off the English, learnt that he had been made High Constable. From 1538, the Abbot of Brantôme, Pierre de Mareuil, had a number of structures built, including a right-angled bridge over the river, an elegant Renaissance house and several resting places in the Monks' garden. His nephew who succeeded him, **Pierre de Bourdeille**, is more well known under the name of Brantôme (cf. biography under Bourdeilles). The abbey was conferred upon him in 1557. On his death, in 1614, **Brantôme** Abbey is the most prosperous in Aquitaine, although it was soon to decline. During the Revolution, its rich library and the last seven monks were dispersed.

The white mass of the abbey and **Saint-Pierre church** border the Dronne and Boulevard Charlemagne. The church, which has both Gothic and Romanesque aspects, has a double-bay nave, crowned with 12th century cupolas, and a type of ribbed vault known as "angevine" from the Gothic period. The building which can be visited today was fully restored in the middle of the last century by the architect Abadie. In the chancel, illuminated by three bay windows, two sculpted wooden panels face each other. A Romanesque capital used as a holy-water basin and a splendid 14th century tablet sculpture featuring the baptism of Christ may also be discovered.

On the north side of the church, the 60 m tall Brantôme **belfry** is unquestionably the finest in Périgord. According to recent studies, it was erected during the Carolingian or even Visigothic period, making it the **oldest belfry in France**. Formed by four recessed storeys, it features **gables** in its upper section. Crowned with a pyramidal stone roof, its various bay-windowed storeys also feature capitals sculpted with an antiquated style of leaves and interweaving.

Only a gallery, a small chapter house with flamboyant arches and ribbed columns, is left of the Renaissance cloisters. Access is gained to the Benedictine abbey, now owned by the village, through this gallery. The 17th century buildings are **open to visitors**. A fine traditional staircase without pillars leads up to two large rooms. In the former monks' dorter, the structural work in the form of an upturned hull is quite remarkable. Various exhibitions are held here. Inside the abbey, a three-part **museum** features significant prehistoric items, furniture and paintings, as well as the strange mediumistic works by the painter and carver Fernand Desmoulin (1857-1914). Saint-Sicaire fountain, said to have fertilising virtues, is concealed behind the abbey as well as **caves** which provide evidence of troglodyte dwellings. One of them includes sculptures of unknown origin, **"The Triumph of Death"** or **"The Last Judgment"** (late 15th century) and **"The Crucifixion"** (16th or 17th century). This cave has been developed into a theatre.

A few metres away, opposite Saint-Roch tower, an elegant **Renaissance house** with transom windows framed with pilasters and colonnettes and whose door is blazoned with the coat of arms of Pierre de Mareuil, guards the little **angled bridge** with starlings which spans the Dronne. The bridge provides a splendid view of the abbey, the paddle-wheel and the foliage of the riverbanks. It also provides access to the public gardens, the former "monks' gardens", where one can relax for a moment on the benches of the grand 16th century **resting places**.

The main town in Northern Périgord for tourism, Brantôme also enjoys a full cultural life which culminates in the summer with the **Festival International de Danse Classique** (ballet) set up in 1958 by Jacqueline Rayet. The "Cave of the Last Judgment" provides a magical setting for this festival, bringing together dancers and 1200 spectators for a millennial rite - the worship of beauty. The abbey also houses the European centre for studies of western spirituality.

One kilometre from the town, a public walk will take you to the fine **Dolmen de la Pierre Levée** (*Dolmen of the Raised Stone*).

Dolmen de la Pierre Levée, Brantôme.

BOURDEILLES
(24 km N.W. of Périgueux)

In a picturesque setting overlooking the Dronne and its village, the enceinte of Bourdeilles in fact encloses a **mediaeval fortress** and a **Renaissance residence**. Historically, the first trace of a Seigneur of Bourdeilles dates back to 1044. He was an important character at the time, **one of the four barons of Périgord**. The fief then was the subject of a number of family quarrels and the barons paid homage in turn to the Abbots of Brantôme, the King of France, the King of England and the Count of Périgord. In 1259, Saint Louis ceded the castle to the English yet, a few years later, **Géraut de Maumont**, counsellor to Philip the Fair, took possession of it and had the mediaeval fortress built between 1283 and 1298. The Renaissance château was the work of Jacquette de Montbron, Brantôme's sister-in-law. She herself drew up the plans for this residence which, according to tradition, was designed to provide accommodation for Catherine de Medici who never came. She died in 1598

before work was completed and without seeing the splendid ceilings which the Italian painter from Fontainebleau school, **Ambroise Le Noble**, decorated during his stay at Bourdeilles, from 1641 to 1644.

Before visiting the castle, let us recall the memory of a person whose name is permanently linked to Bourdeilles, **Pierre de Bourdeilles**, known as **"Brantôme"** (1538-1614), one of Périgord's most famous writers. The family's third son, he was quite naturally destined for the clergy. In 1557, Henry II granted him the benefits of Brantôme Abbey. Having little taste for religious life, he was never ordained priest. He travelled far and wide, firstly to Italy in 1558 and 1559. Then he accompanied the wretched Queen of France, Mary Stuart, in her Scottish exile in 1561. A brief stay in the court of Charles IX and there he was, fighting alongside François de Guise against the Protestants before setting off on new ventures. In 1564, he enrolled in the Spanish army and went to fight in **Morocco,** then regained **Portugal.** The year of 1566 saw our abbot take part in the **Maltese** crusade

Bourdeilles mill.

Bourdeilles Castle: entrance and watch tower. A medieval castle and a Renaissance house stand behind these walls.

Facing page: Bourdeilles, the mediaeval castle and 38 m octagonal dungeon.

Grand-Brassac: decorations on the northern portal of the fortress church. Beneath the semicircular arch: the adoration of the Three Wise Men. Above, Christ between Saint John and the Virgin Mary, flanked by Saint Peter and another saint difficult to identify.

against the Turks. He may at that time have been considered something of a **pirate.** He waged war all over France until 1569 when illness forced him to spend almost a year at his abbey. A true conquistador, he then prepared an expedition to **Peru** but the project fell through. In 1582, after the death of his elder brother, he saw himself dispossessed of his inheritance and Henry III refused him the title of Seneschal of Périgord. He then dreamt of betraying his country in favour of Spain but a serious fall from a horse crippled him. Broken physically, if not morally, he resided from 1583 to 1587 at Brantôme Abbey or at Richemont Castle which he had had built, and devoted all his energy to writing. After a short stay at the court, he retired to the country for good. He died on 5th July 1614 at **Richemont castle** (16th-17th century), **now open to visitors** (see Brantôme's tomb, with its curious decor of heads, interlocking tibias and tears of silver). His works were published only after his death, in Leyden, Holland. Today, his two most well-known works are *Les Vies des Hommes Illustres et des Grands Capitaines* and his masterpiece, ***Les Dames Galantes***, a collection of stimulating portraits and lively, spicy tales.

Ribérac: Notre-Dame collegiate college (12th century).

Bourdeilles Castle, which has belonged to the département since 1960, is **open to visitors**. From the entrance, flanked by two machicolated round towers from the 15th century, one perceives the Renaissance arcade of the Seneschal's entrance and the portal of the oratory. On the right, we come to the terreplein where the castle and château stand. The fortress built by Géraud de Maumont, counsellor to Philip the Fair, at the end of the 13th century, was altered in the 15th. On the site of former mediaeval houses, one may visit a cobblestone courtyard, with its well, surrounded by high walls. Featuring bay windows with ledges, they are surmounted by parapet walks overlooked by the impressive 38 metre **octagonal dungeon**, erected in the early 14th century, justifiably considered the finest in Périgord. Here we discover *oubliettes* and three floors with ribbed vaults and illuminated by loopholes. A spiral staircase takes us to the crenellated summit which provides a view of the whole of Bourdeilles. In the buildings adjacent to the tower, we are able to admire, on the first floor, a vast room with a semicircular arch, cobblestone paving and a 13th century gemel bay window. The Renaissance mansion, converted into a **museum**, contains an interesting **collection of furniture** from the 16th and 17th centuries, mostly originating from Burgundy and Spain, as well as a number of pieces of armour and works of art — a reproduction of the Bayeux tapestry, a magnificent 16th century entombment of eight figures, a 13th century wooden statue of Christ, etc. In the first floor dining room with its Renaissance fireplace, the walls are decorated with 15th and 18th century tapestries and portraits. The masterpiece of Bourdeilles is the **golden drawing-room** (*salon doré*) measuring 15 x 10 m, which features monumental fireplaces, and ceilings and wooden panelling decorated by Ambroise Le Noble. It contains a rich selection of furniture and beautiful 16th and 17th century tapestries. Every summer, the château provides the venue for remarkable exhibitions.

RIBÉRAC

(37 km west of Périgueux)

On the northern edge of the marshy Double forest lies the charming little town of **Ribérac**, where Notre-Dame church must be seen. Ribérac has retained the memory of the famous troubadour **Arnaud Daniel**, songster of the "trobar clus" (esoteric poetry), "Arnaud who cries and goes on singing", praised by Dante, Petrarch and Aragon. Near Ribérac, we shall see the curious Roman tower of **La Rigale Castle** and **Comberanche** hospital commandery (14th-17th century).

The interesting aspect of the Ribérac area for tourists resides in its trail of **Romanesque churches with cupolas**, the finest in Périgord. To the south of Ribérac, we shall discover **Saint Martin** (12th century, two cupolas), **Segonzac** (11th century, sculpted capitals), **Siorac** (12th century, fortified, cupolas) and **Saint-André-de-Double** (12th and 14th century, fortified). To the northeast, the fortress church of **Grand-Brassac** (12th century), with its three cupolas and sculpted portal is a pure masterpiece. We shall also see **Celles** (12th century, fortified), **Paussac** and **Saint-Vivien** churches and the ruins of **La-Tour-Blanche Castle**. To the north of Ribérac, these include **Allemans** (Romanesque, fortified), **Cherval** (11th-12th century), one of the finest with its four cupolas, sculptures and fortifications, **Vendoire** (sculpted Saintonge façade) and **Bouteilles** (austere fortress).

To the west, a visit to the churches in **Saint-Privat-des-Prés** (12th century, highly fortified) and **Aubeterre** (Romanesque **monolith**, formerly in Périgord, now in Charentes) is an absolute must. In the surrounding area, we shall see the churches in **Festalemps** (cupolas, fortified) and **Vanxains** (11th-12th century, asymmetric plan, fortified and sculpted). Visitors should also see the **Sauteranne** alignment in Vanxains, Bourg-du-Bost, Ponteyraud and Saint-Antoine-Cumond and, further south, the fine churches in **Saint-Aulaye** (sculpted Saintonge façade) and **Cheneaud** (12th century, sculptures).

Vanxains and its fortified church.

Purple Périgord

Grape harvest in the Bergerac region.

The Bergerac country is first and foremost a land of vineyards.
Are we still in Périgord or now in the Bordeaux region? We are in Purple Périgord
(Périgord Pourpre), a landscape of low slopes covered with tight rows of vines.
A land of good living which also saw the greatest French philosophers,
Michel de Montaigne and Maine de Biran, grow and mature on its soil.

Bergerac bridge, over the Dordogne.

Cyrano de Bergerac.

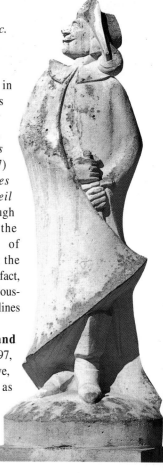

BERGERAC

Bergerac, the second-largest town in Dordogne (30,000 inhabitants), is the capital of south-west Périgord, a district which opens out on to the Bordeaux region which might be termed the land of the vineyard or **Purple Périgord**. Bergerac is an active industrial centre with, in particular, the national powder factory, one of the largest firms in Périgord. It is also the site of the large research centre for the *Institut National des Tabacs* (tobacco) of which Dordogne is a major producer. Finally, its intellectual role is not insignificant. But here, **vines** dominate the economy as much as the landscape. The 100,000 acres of vineyards produce 75 % of Dordogne's production. The cellar of every **"wine cooperative"** offers its precious beverage for tasting, particularly the Bergerac and Monbazillac cellars which are **open to visitors**. The wines of Bergerac are, from north-east to north-west, **Pécharmant**, one of the most highly appreciated by connoisseurs, the fruity **Rosette**, the white and red **Côtes-de-Bergerac** and the mellow white **Montravel**, already enjoyed by Montaigne. To the south, we find **Monbazillac**, the most well known and, around Sigoulès, **Saussignac**, praised by Rabelais.

It should be admitted that the most famous "son" of Bergerac never experienced "the gentle green of evening on the Dordogne". Indeed, the philosopher, essayist and playwright

Savinien de Cyrano (born in Paris in 1619, died in Sannois [Val d'Oise] in 1655), author of *La Mort d'Agrippine, Histoires Comiques des États et Empires de la Lune* (1657) and *Histoires Comiques des États et Empires du Soleil* (1662), was a Parisian through and through. On entering the company of the *Cadets* of Gascony, he naturally took the name of Bergerac. He held, in fact, the fief of "Bergerac" (now Sous-Forêts), near Dampierre, Yvelines (Paris region).

It was **Edmond Rostand** who, in his famous play of 1897, made him a Gascon full of verve, with a legendary nose, and as skilful a swordsman as he was a poet. In his drama, he used characters who actually existed in the life of the real Cyrano.

The quaint old areas of Bergerac.

Similarly, his strange death seems quite authentic. But let's console ourselves. Even if Cyrano was not from Périgord, at least he made the name of Bergerac well known throughout the world. We should also mention the philosopher **Maine de Biran** who lived at Grateloup Castle in the Pécharmant vineyards.

The history of Bergerac since the Middle Ages can be summed up in three words: the river, the wine and the bridge. Even though the Dordogne was used as a passage by the Barbarian, Arab and Viking invaders to penetrate inland, it was above all a channel for economic development. Bergerac became an important **barge port** governing the river traffic between Auvergne and the Bordeaux region. Bergerac being situated on the road to Santiago de Compostela, a bridge was built towards the ninth century, around which the town gradually developed. Bergerac wines had already begun to refresh English and Dutch throats at this time. In 1254, quarrels over the succession of the Rudel house, owner of the town, allowed the English to establish a foothold in western Périgord. The intervention of Du Guesclin was required to free the city. Bergerac was declared a free town,

that is to say it was not subject to the authority of a seigneur, as early as the 12th century, but consular power was not to be effectively constituted for another century. By 1545, the **Calvinist faith** made deep inroads into the intellectual and bourgeois milieus under the influence of the Queen of Navarre and her court, installed in the nearby town of Nérac.

Château de Lanquais bears the traces of the bombardment inflicted upon it by Henri de La Tour-d'Auvergne in 1577.

Bergerac welcomed Jeanne d'Albret and her son, Henry of Navarre, with open arms in 1568. After the massacre of St Bartholomew (1572), it became, in the words of Pierre Barrière, **"the intellectual capital of the Protestant world"**. But in 1620, the town was invested by Royal troops and Richelieu had the ramparts razed in 1629. Several Huguenots then emigrated to Holland and England.

The old city is outlined by the river and Rue Saint-Esprit, Rue Neuve-d'Argenson and Rue de la Résistance, dug out along the lines of the former ramparts. Close to the former convent of the Ladies of Faith, converted into the Town Hall, **Peyrarède House** or Henry IV Château is the site of the **Tobacco museum**, the only one in France, which traces the history of "Nicot's weed", imported in the 16th century. By 1674, tobacco farming was already regulated in France. The monopoly set up in 1816 restricted the production of this plant to the Agen region, Périgord and Quercy. The museum consists of four parts, the history of tobacco, a presentation of related techniques (farming, manufacture, marketing), a collection of smoker's objects and finally works of art (paintings, chinaware) which have the common theme of tobacco. Peyrarède House is also the site of the **local history museum** which includes an interesting section devoted to prehistory.

The former **Les Récollets Convent** has preserved two wings of its cloisters. **Open to visitors**, this building which places architectural elements from the 14th and 17th centuries side by side, is the headquarters of the *Conseil Interprofessionnel des Vins* (wine trade association) for the Bergerac region. Receptions and the "enthronement" of the wine crops take place here.

Rue de la Myrpe, one of the most pleasant in the town, is lined with old half-timbered houses, occasionally with cob walls. Rue des Conférences owes its name to the Bergerac peace treaty (1577), reached between the King of Navarre and representatives of Henry III, which put an end to the Sixth War

of Religion. Here we find a wine and **river transport museum.** Having admired the fountain in Place Pelissière, we reach Saint-Jacques church, to which reference was made in the tenth century and which acted as a stage on the road to Compostela. Destroyed during the Wars of Religion, it was restored in the 19th century but has retained its belfry and flamboyant windows. A museum of sacred art is located nearby.

Rue Saint-James with its 15th and 16th century residences and Rue des Fontaines, with its "old inn" from the 14th century, form an attractive area which makes for a pleasant stroll. On the Place du Marché, the "Charles IX house" received a visit by that very king on 8th August 1565.

To the north of Bergerac, we shall visit the cavalry museum in **Campsegret**. Further up the Dordogne, **Château de Lanquais** (15th-17th century), open to visitors, was the property of the beautiful **Ysabeau de Limeuil**, a member of the Catherine de Medici's "flying squadron". On the opposite bank, **Château de Baneuil** (13th-15th century) can also be visited. Continuing a little further up the river, we shall discover the **Couze** paper mills (visits) and the bastide of **Lalinde** (panoramic view from Saint-Front Chapel).

Lalinde Gate, the remains of the fortifications of the bastide.

Monbazillac Castle. The Huguenots worshipped here.

Overleaf: The Monbazillac vineyards.

MONBAZILLAC
(6 km south of Bergerac)

Erected in the heart of the vines, right next to the village, **Monbazillac Castle**, which is **open to visitors**, was built around 1550 by François d'Aydie and his wife Françoise de Salignac, and completed by Charles d'Aydie and Jeanne de Bourdeille. It managed to survive the Wars of Religion and the Fronde without damage. Being practically untouched since the Renaissance era, it has retained a great deal of authenticity. The façade of the house, which is cornered by four large round towers, features transom windows. A crenellated parapet walk surmounted by high gable windows, goes around the whole castle. The red tile roof which covers the grey stone building has lilied weather-vanes. Dry moats complement the defensive system of this château which, although built in the 16th century, has a distinctly mediaeval character.

Owned by the Monbazillac wine cooperative, the castle contains a number of **museums**. The main room with its French-style ceiling has a monumental 16th century fireplace and two 17th century tapestries from Flanders. In the various rooms, one may discover Périgord-style furniture, old engravings and cards, medals, drawings by **Sem**, a local caricaturist from the early 20th century, and the history of Protestantism in the Bergerac region, the castle having long been used as a temple. On the first floor, the Louis XIII bedroom of the Viscountess of Monbazillac has been recreated. The **cellars** naturally house a wine museum (a **tasting** room which offers visitors the chance to purchase directly from the château). One might also take a stroll in the ten-acre grounds and discover the wide panorama over the vineyards and the Bergerac valley from the terraces.

Anyone who is fond of good wine will recognise Monbazillac Castle on the labels of the region's most well-known vintage. The **vineyard** which produces a fortified white wine, sweet yet suitably fruity, covers around 7500 acres. Created by monks in the 11th century, it experienced strong growth in the 17th century with the increase in exports to Holland. **Château de Bridoire** (15th century) which belonged to the family of Father Charles de Foucauld must also be seen.

SAINT-MICHEL-DE-MONTAIGNE
and MONTCARET

(41 km west of Bergerac)

On the border between Gironde and Dordogne, in a **castle (open to visitors)** surrounded by vineyards producing a sweet white wine, Montravel, enjoyed by the philosopher, the most famous son of Périgord and one of humanity's outstanding thinkers, **Michel de Montaigne** (1533-1592), awaits us. The progeny, on his father's side, of a family of ennobled merchants and, on his mother's side, of descendants of rich Spanish Jews, Montaigne was born at the castle on 28th February 1533. In 1554, as his father was Mayor of Bordeaux, he was named counsellor at the Court of Aids of Périgueux at the age of 21. He entered the Bordeaux parliament in 1557 where he became the friend of **Étienne de La Boëtie**, his senior by three years. This exemplary friendship with the one whom Montaigne considered his master of thought lasted six years until the death of La Boëtie on 18th August 1563. On 22nd September 1565, he married Françoise de La Chassaigne who was to give him six daughters. Sadly only one of them survived. On the death of his father in 1568, he became the seigneur of Montaigne and made strong representations for its adherence to Périgord. In a parody of Caesar, he wrote "and would hold me in greater esteem, at a venture, second or third in Périgueux than first in Paris". Having sold his parliament office, he withdrew to the countryside in 1571. The following year, the year of the massacre of St Bartholomew, he began to **write** his *Essais*. Until 1580, he left his castle on very few occasions and although Henry of Navarre made him a gentleman of the Privy Chamber, he devoted his time to writing the first two parts of his work. The first edition of Essais appeared on 1st March 1580. Montaigne went up to Paris to present his book to Henry III, then set out on a **long journey** throughout France, Switzerland and Italy. On 7th September 1581, in Lucca, he learnt that he had been appointed **Mayor of Bordeaux** for two years and returned to Montaigne by 30th November. During his two successive terms of office, whilst continuing to correct his *Essais,* Montaigne distinguished himself by his **tolerance** and his desire to keep the peace. In December 1584, he welcomed the

Michel de Montaigne's "Library" where he wrote his Essais.

future Henry IV to his castle and, the following year, the plague chased him out of the town. Retiring to his castle, he devoted himself only to writing, in spite of his rest being disturbed by the visit of Le Béarnais in 1587, in the wake of the Battle of Coutras. While still working on revising his *Essais* to which he devoted twenty years of his life, Montaigne passed away in his castle on 13th September 1592.

After being ravaged by a fire in the 19th century, **Montaigne Castle** was rebuilt in a neo-Renaissance style which can barely be described as lack-lustre. Having passed the gate and entering a courtyard enclosed by ramparts, we discover the only vestige of the 16th century and the object of numerous literary pilgrimages, the round tower, the **"Library"**, joined by a turret staircase to a tall square house. On the ground floor, we find the chapel and the alcove from which Montaigne followed the services. A spiral staircase and a low door provide access to the upper floor, the library, a spartan room heated by a single fireplace, of which the **beams** and joists bear some **54** painted and carved stoic, Epicurean and sceptical **mottoes in Greek and Latin**, a real synthesis of Montaigne's thinking. The

memory of the philosopher has been retained in the landscape discovered through the windows — the path where he used to stroll and the façade where he had planned to have a peaceful parapet walk built specifically for the purpose of walking. Nearby, we shall visit the Gallo-Roman **Montcaret Villa**, which was succeeded by a Merovingian priory.

Overleaf: The hamlet of Pech-Saint-Sourd, between Les Eyzies and Le Bugue.

The Gallo-Roman mosaics of Montcaret Villa.

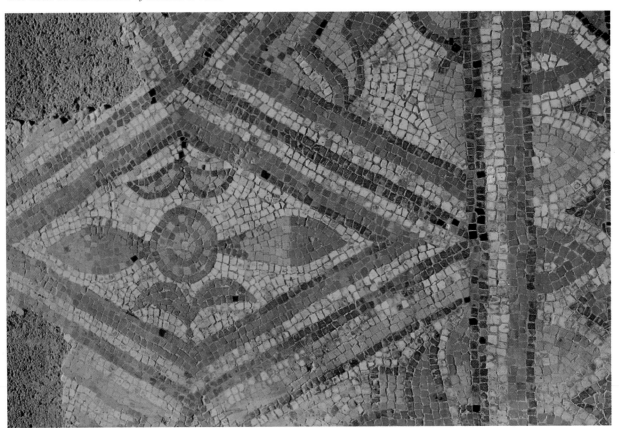

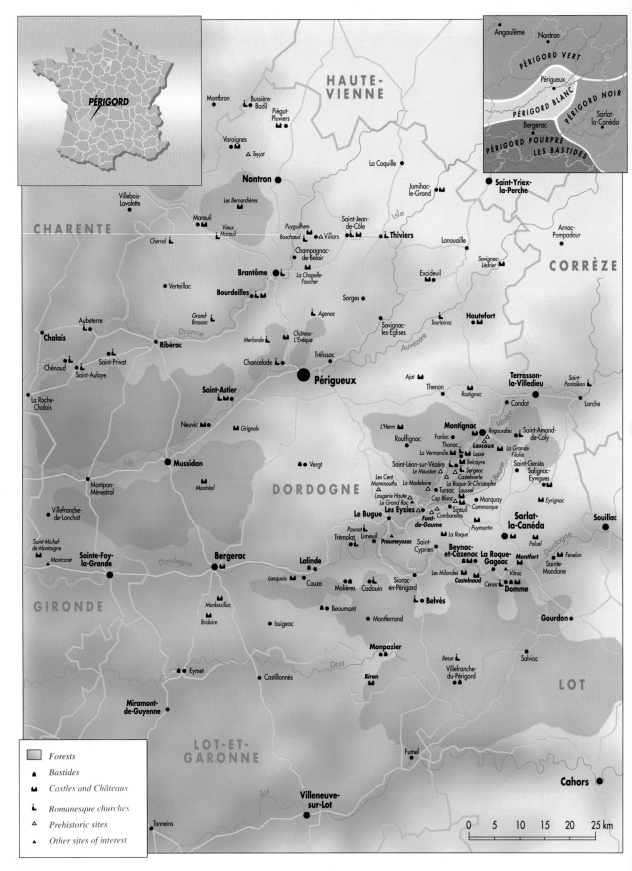

PÉRIGORD

Montbron
Bussière-Badil
Piégut-Pluviers
HAUTE-VIENNE
Varaignes
△ Teyjat
La Coquille
Saint-Yriex-la-Perche
Jumihac-le-Grand
Villebois-Lavalette
Nontron
Les Bernardières
CHARENTE
Mareuil
Vieux Mareuil
Puyguilhem
Saint-Jean-de-Côle
Isle
Cherval
Boschaud △ Villars
Saint-Léon-sur-Vézère
Thiviers
Lanouaille
Arnac-Pompadour
Champagnac-de-Belair
CORRÈZE
Brantôme
Verteillac
La Chapelle-Faucher
Excideuil
Savignac-Lédrier
Bourdeilles
Grand-Brassac
Sorges
Agonac
Savignac-les-Eglises
Hautefort
Chalais
Aubeterre
Merlande
Château-L'Evêque
Tourtoirac
Terrasson-la-Villedieu
Saint-Pantaléon
Ribérac
Dronne
Trélissac
Auvézère
Saint-Privat
Chancelade
Chénaud
Saint-Aulaye
Périgueux
Ajat
Thenon
Condat
Larche
La Roche-Chalais
Saint-Astier
Rastignac
L'Herm
Montignac
Regourdou
Saint-Amand-de-Coly
Neuvic
Grignols
Rouffignac
Fanlac
Lascaux
La Grande Filolie
Thonac
Mussidan
Vergt
Saint-Léon-sur-Vézère
La Vermondie
Losse
Belcayre
Saint-Geniès
Salignac-Eyvigues
Montpon-Ménestrol
Montréal
DORDOGNE
Le Moustier △
Sergeac
Castelmerle
Les Cent Mammouths
La Madeleine
La Roque-St-Christophe
Villefranche-de-Lonchat
Laugerie Haute
Le Grand Roc
Cap Blanc
Laussel
Marquay
Eyrignac
Saint-Michel-de-Montaigne
Montcaret
Sainte-Foy-la-Grande
Le Bugue
Les Eyzies
Font-de-Gaume
Sireuil
Combarelles
Commarque
Sarlat-Canéda
Souillac
Bergerac
Paunat
Trémolat
Limeuil
Proumeyssac
Saint-Cyprien
La Roque
Puymartin
Beynac-et-Cazenac
La Roque-Gageac
Montfort
Paluel
Fénelon
GIRONDE
Dordogne
Lalinde
Lanquais
Couze
Molières
Cadouin
Siorac-en-Périgord
Castelnaud
Les Milandes
Vitrac
Cénac
Domme
Sainte-Mondane
Monbazillac
Bridoire
Beaumont
Issigeac
Montferrand
Belvès
Gourdon
GARONNE
Eymet
Castillonnès
Drot
Monpazier
Biron
Besse
Villefranche-du-Périgord
Salviac
LOT
Miramont-de-Guyenne
Fumel
LOT-ET-GARONNE
Cahors
Villeneuve-sur-Lot
Lot
Tonneins

ANGOULÊME Nontron
PÉRIGORD VERT
Périgueux
PÉRIGORD BLANC
PÉRIGORD NOIR
Sarlat-la-Canéda
Bergerac
PÉRIGORD POURPRE
LES BASTIDES

Forests
Bastides
Castles and Châteaux
Romanesque churches
△ Prehistoric sites
Other sites of interest

0   5   10   15   20   25 km

Vézère Valley, the birthplace of Prehistory.

The chestnut market in Villefranche-du-Périgord.

Truffles, the black diamonds of Périgord.

The fortified church in Tayac.

Beynac Castle.

TABLE OF CONTENTS

Photographic credits:
Andia/B. Peyencet: p.7 centre. Andia/S. Corre: p.59 bottom right and p.68 centre. Andia/A. Galy: p.101 top left, p.102 top right and bottom right and p.113 bottom. Nicolas Fediaevsky: p.30 bottom, p.37 bottom, p.44 bottom, p.50 and p.83 top left. Editions La Goélette, Paris: p.48 bottom and p.49. Hervé Champollion: p.55 bottom, p.58, p. 59 top, p.60 bottom, p.66 top left and bottom.
Map: *Philippe Rekacewicz and Cécile Marin.*

Cet ouvrage a été imprimé par l'imprimerie Pollina à Luçon (85) - n° 71222
I.S.B.N. 2.7373.1771.1 – Dépôt légal : mars 1996
N° d'éditeur : 3160.02.1,5.01.97